TEACH YOURSELF BOOKS

SWIMMING

Some other Teach Yourself Books

TEACH YOURSELF BOOKS

SWIMMING

Frank Waterman

TEACH YOURSELF BOOKS

ST PAUL'S HOUSE   WARWICK LANE   LONDON   EC4

First Printed 1953
This Edition 1970

SBN 340 05732 7

Printed in Great Britain for The English Universities Press Ltd by
Elliott Bros. & Yeoman Ltd., Liverpool

CONTENTS

ACKNOWLEDGEMENTS

The author and publishers express their thanks to The Royal Life Saving Society for permission to use certain material from their handbook in the final chapter of this work, and to The Amateur Swimming Association for the use of extracts from the rules of Water Polo, including the diagram of the field of play.

They also thank G. H. ATKINSON, R. G. UNDERWOOD, R. F. WINDRIDGE, JOHN L. NEALE and COLOUR/SGT. B. J. STOKES, R.M. for expert assistance with other parts of the text and in the preparation of the diagrams.

CHAPTER I

How to Begin

Most four-footed animals, like the dog or the horse, can swim at their first attempt, merely by performing their accustomed movements of running. Man, on the other hand, having long ago ceased to run on all fours, finds the process of learning to swim somewhat artificial and involved. He may, of course, learn to 'dog-paddle' and this without difficulty—many people in fact have started swimming in this way—but this stroke, if it can be called a stroke, is cumbersome and will not get him far. So nowadays the dog-paddle is really only used as a kind of introductory exercise to the much more refined and desirable 'Front Crawl'.

Yet if the learning process is more difficult for us humans, it is certain that the rewards are much more worth while, for to swim easily and confidently, in good style and with a variety of strokes, is a source of real and lasting joy for young and old alike. In swimming, as in all branches of sport, one's pleasure in performance increases with one's ability to appreciate and experience the finer points of the game. Also we might mention here—although we may repeat it later on—to swim in good style means not only to swim gracefully or elegantly but also to swim faster. In other words, one of the results of good style swimming is that of securing maximum return of speed for a minimum expenditure of energy.

It might also be mentioned here, at the very beginning of this instructional book, that because of its range and variety of movement the practice of swimming and diving

I

is a healthy and wholesome form of exercise which may make large and important contributions to one's physical development and well-being. For these, and many other, reasons, it will pay you, the reader, to learn this game of swimming as thoroughly as possible, coming with me step by step through the many interesting adventures in movement, until you reach that much envied stage of skill which delights both the performer and the spectator. It is appreciated that for many would-be swimmers the services of a trained and experienced coach are quite beyond their reach, and it is for such as these, whether young or old, that this book has been written.

The General Idea

Let us get away on the correct foot and decide straight away how we intend you, the reader, should 'teach yourself swimming.' In the first place, I am going to assume that you, as my pupil, are eager to learn and willing to give some time to the serious study and practice of the subject. The method I shall employ as your swimming coach is what we might call the 'easy stages' method. By this I mean that:

(1) We shall first examine the movement or stroke as a whole, with the idea of providing a complete 'mind picture' of what the stroke really looks like.

(2) We shall then, with this picture in mind, first examine and then practise each part of the stroke—the arm movements, the leg, the breathing, and so on.

(3) When we have mastered these movements separately, first on land and then in the water, we shall begin to connect them up, link by link, until the full chain or the complete stroke has been mastered.

Advantage of Working with a Partner

I have some sympathy for the boy or girl who may get

impatient over this slow methodical 'easy stages' method, but I must emphasise—and I shall keep on emphasising—that real success will come only to those of you who are prepared to curb your natural desires to jump your fences or skip your practices. In learning to swim, it is so easy to acquire bad habits of movement which, as a rule, take far longer to eradicate than they take to form. For this reason, although it is not essential, it is a good thing to team up with a partner and assist one another, both in the water practices and in some of the land exercises, by giving manual support when it is needed and by being always on the look-out for faulty movements. If your partner is already a swimmer, all the better for you; if not, you will both find it great fun to learn the game together.

The value of having the assistance of a partner while learning becomes more obvious when your water practice has to be done in the sea, for you cannot concentrate fully on the work in hand when your mind is frequently distracted by waves and tides and the risk of getting out of your depth. At such times a partner standing near is a great psychological and practical help.

Home Preparation

Much of your learning can be done at home, for you can read and study the descriptions of the various strokes, plan your lessons for your next visit to the pool or sea-shore, and, by following the suggestions on 'land exercises,' do much to prepare the way for your mastery of the actual swimming movements. I know personally of at least one case when a boy of twelve years of age, who had never been in a swimming pool before, spent three winter months learning the various 'land drills' in a school gymnasium at odd times. Then, when the pool was opened in May, he walked straight down the steps into the water and proceeded to swim the width! While no doubt many such cases could be quoted, such an encouraging result is exceptional; but it does at least show what can be cone if you are keen enough and if you have confidence in yourself and your instructor.

I am confident that, by following the instructions on 'land exercises' carefully, making sure that you really master each stage before passing on to the next, you will find it possible to build up most of the swimming strokes, with all their difficult co-ordinations, even before you practise them in the water.

You will notice that, as you swim your way through this book, I have planned your lessons so that each phase of water practice is preceded by a series of land exercises for home preparation. The object of this arrangement is to enable you to prepare for your water practices so that every moment of your time in the water may be spent to the best advantage.

Artificial Aids

Nowadays, there are many and varied artificial aids which, if used properly, can be of great use in the early stages of your learning to swim campaign. The great advantage of using these artificial aids is that you can raise your feet off the bottom of the bath and get the feeling of propelling yourself through the water on your very first visit to the swimming bath.

Worth particular mention are the inflatable rings which fit over the upper arms. It is impossible for them to slip off and they will keep even the heaviest adult afloat with his head out of the water. They are particularly useful when carrying out for the first few times some of the confidence exercises mentioned in Chapter III. Once you have mastered these exercises with the help of your floats, try the exercises without them, and in a surprisingly short time you will feel at home in the water.

As soon as you have learnt the arm and leg movements of the various strokes, your floats will help you to co-ordinate these movements without the fear of sinking.

Polystyrene floats can be used with advantage as, for example, when a swimmer wishes to improve his leg action by the well-established method of grasping a float with arms stretched out in front of him.

A word of warning is necessary here, however. Whenever you are using any type of swimming aid, always remain in water where you are able to stand up. These aids, remember, are for the purpose of helping you to learn to swim on your own; they are not a means of supporting you in the water while you play about.

Some Dangers to Avoid

Learning to swim imposes an obligation on the learner not only to avoid risking his own life but also that of his would-be rescuer. There is probably no need for me to stress this point, but a few words on some of the commonest dangers which the learner can avoid may not be out of place:

1 If you are susceptible to cramp, do not go in the water unless the temperature is at least 65°, and do not go in within two hours of a substantial meal or enter the the water when you are very hot.

2 Never go swimming from the sea-shore when the tide is on the ebb, that is to say, running out.

3 Always keep within your depth until you have the confidence and ability to swim at least a hundred yards.

4 Remember that beaches vary and that some have dangerous undercurrents and steep and sudden falls.

5 If you are learning to swim in a river, avoid weeds. Try to get a safe area roped off and keep within this; and make sure that the water is not polluted but is safe for an occasional mouthful!

CHAPTER II

Elementary Principles

A comparison of the styles of good swimmers with those of the novice or beginner shows certain obvious differences. Perhaps the most striking is the fact that the good swimmer seems to move easily and gracefully through the water and at the same time obtains a greater return of speed for his outlay of energy. On the other hand, the novice gives the impression that he is struggling against a force which is for ever trying to make him sink and to fill his mouth, nostrils and eyes with water. The expert cleaves the water with regular movements in a smooth, even rhythm; he has no trouble with his breathing and he seems to be lying comfortably in the water. The novice, however, uses his arms like windmills, creates a great deal of splash, and expends a considerable amount of energy to very little purpose.

Every swimming stroke, whether it is breast, crawl or back crawl, has its own specialised techniques. These have been carefully worked out by the experts and have been standardised in the process of developing styles which are not only pleasing to the eye of the spectator but are also best for competition purposes. What, then, are the rules of good style in swimming? Let us consider some of them separately.

1 The Rule of Relaxation

To understand this rule, we must first appreciate one or two simple facts of physiology. For example, when a muscle is contracted or tensed, it burns up more fuel or energy than when it is relaxed; it can only survive constant tension for a limited time before tiring. Yet by alternately contracting and relaxing *in an even rhythm* a muscle can sustain action over a much longer period; that is to say, it recovers during its brief periods of rest.

Now most beginners at swimming use far too much energy by tensing their muscles and making their movements too rapid. The good swimmer, however, is the one who has learned to relax in the water and to use his arms and legs in an easy rhythm of work and rest, work and rest. This rule of relaxation—or of economy of effort—is applicable to all swimming strokes, and once the pupil has mastered its meaning and has applied it to his own swimming, he will be well on the way to success.

For the time being, let us remember just this—overtenseness in swimming, as in any other athletic activity, makes for clumsy, awkward movements and quickly leads to fatigue. In all your lessons in swimming, therefore, remember always to make your movements as smooth as possible, relaxing your muscles whenever the opportunity occurs.

2 The Principle of Correct Body Poise

Without being too technical, I must remind the reader that water is more dense than air and that if he were to attempt to run in it, that is, in an upright position with only his head above the surface, he would make very slow progress. If, however, he were able to float horizontally on the surface of the water, it would require only a slight force to move him along, either head first or feet first. Look at diagrams 1*a* and 1*b*.

Diagram 1*a* represents a board being pulled through water in the direction of the arrow. It will be seen that the whole of its front surface is being pulled against the resistance of the water. It is easy to realise that a considerable force is required to overcome such resistance. Diagram 1*b*

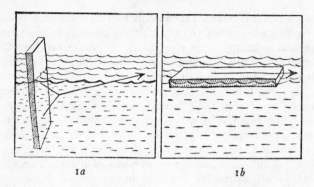

1a   1b

shows the same board floating horizontally in the water. Movement in the direction of the arrow is met by only slight resistance, that corresponding to the thickness of the board, in fact. In this case, very little force is needed to move the object. If, in place of the board, we imagine a person, we must agree that there is only one position for a swimmer who wishes to travel quickly, and that is the horizontal one. In other words, *it is a fault of style to allow the legs to sink below the body and so cause a drag.*

There is another good reason why this rule is important. If the swimmer's body is in an inclined and not a horizontal position, the force of his leg drive is very largely wasted in attempting to lift his body out of the water. On the other hand, with the body in the horizontal position, any propelling force which comes from the legs and feet is utilised to the very best advantage in driving the body forward. The thing to remember, then, is—*streamline the body and always keep your legs well up.*

3 The Principle of Correct Timing

Every cycle of movements constituting a swimming stroke must be co-ordinated in such a way as to secure the maximum momentum from the minimum expenditure of energy. For example, in the Breast Stroke the two main factors in propulsion are the Arm Pull and the Leg Drive If these two forces were applied together, the result would be a sudden spurt or leap, followed by an almost complete check during the period of preparation for the next stroke. If, however, these forces are applied separately, the momentum derived from each will be carried over to the next. Furthermore, it is possible by this method to ensure that when each force is applied, the rest of the body is maintained in a position which offers least resistance to progress. The rule may be illustrated diagrammatically as follows:

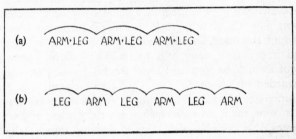

(a) ARM·LEG ARM·LEG ARM·LEG

(b) LEG ARM LEG ARM LEG ARM

2

Line (a) represents a series of three Breast Strokes in which the arm and leg movements are performed together, while line (b) indicates the same number of strokes but with the arm and leg movements performed independently. It will be seen that for the same expenditure of energy, the swimmer travels further in a given time—that is, faster —with method (b) than with with method (a). Another useful illustration is that of the car engine—imagine what would happen if all four or six cylinders fired together!

4 The Principle of Regular Breathing
Every swimming cycle should be accompanied by a full

breathing cycle—inhalation and exhalation. There are three advantages to be gained from this rule:

(a) It enables the swimmer to sustain muscular effort by ensuring a regular supply of oxygen to the lungs, and thence to the muscles, thereby offsetting fatigue.

(b) It reduces strain on the heart.

(c) It assists in the general co-ordination of the stroke cycle, and in that way makes for grace and ease of movement.

Summary

The above four important principles—relaxation, body poise, timing and regular breathing—form the basis of all good swimming. The beginner can hardly be expected to appreciate them fully, but as he proceeds on his way through this book, he will gradually realise their significance and importance more and more. Then, if he can make them form a background basis for his strokes, he will be rewarded with a smooth even rhythm which will more than compensate him for all his trouble. At the moment, though, it is sufficient if he *understands* these principles; as he progresses, this understanding should develop into a valuable practical application.

CHAPTER III

Gaining Confidence in the Water

Before you are able to swim even one breadth of your swimming bath you have quite a lot to learn. Probably your most important lesson is on making friends with the water. Water is an element which can drown a person; it is often uncomfortably cold; it has a way of getting into one's eyes, nose, mouth and ears; and when one is unused to it—and especially when it comes in waves—it is extremely difficult even to stand or walk in it, let alone swim in it. Incidentally 'fear of water' is very often a 'fear of *cold* water,' and first attempts should always be made in a well-heated pool.

So before we attempt to swim, let us spend some time and thought in getting to understand the water; it will well repay us. First of all, let us appreciate the fact that water is buoyant, that is to say, it possesses the power of supporting objects or keeping things up. So far as we are concerned, it is sufficient at present to know that water is capable of holding us up, provided we do not struggle and provided we keep sufficient air in our lungs. To illustrate this important and fundamental principle, here are some useful practices which you can carry out at home.

A Breathing Exercise

Before we pass on to the actual study of swimming strokes, let us try out an experiment in breathing which will make a very useful contribution to our equipment for learning to swim. We might try this in the wash basin at home.

Fill the basin to within about three inches of the rim and lean over so as to submerge your face to your ears. Practise breathing out under water in various ways, first through the nostrils only, then through the mouth only, and finally through the nostrils and mouth together. The result of this simple experiment should prove to you:

(a) That breathing out through the nostrils is possible, but not easy or pleasant.

(b) That breathing out through the mouth permits a certain amount of water to enter the nostrils, which again is unpleasant, and

(c) That breathing out through nostrils and mouth simultaneously not only keeps the nostrils clear of water but also enables the breath to be expelled without undue force.

Now let us try another experiment, this time connected with inhaling. From the same position as before—that is, with face submerged—breathe out and then turn your head sideways to bring your mouth just out of the water, while keeping one side of your face still submered. Now breathe in, first one way then another as before—first nostrils, then mouth, then both together. What is the result? You will discover that the best way to breathe in is through the mouth only. Remember this rule, then, for future application in all cases when your head has to be partly submerged while you are swimming: *Breathe in through the mouth and out through the nose and mouth.*

Let us now go a stage further. Submerge your face under water and breathe out through the mouth and nose. Then turn your head to the side and breathe in, through the mouth only. Repeat this as many times as you can, keeping to a nice steady rhythm. Whenever you go to the bath or the beach, always spend a few minutes on this exercise; the time spent will be amply rewarded later on.

Confidence Practice No. 1

If you are short enough or if your bath is long enough, try to float on your back with your fingertips just resting on the bottom of the bath. Notice what little support is needed to keep you afloat, and notice also how your body rises and falls with your breathing.

These two simple practices should convince you of the following facts:

1 Water is buoyant and under certain circumstances will hold you up.

2 If your lungs are full of air, it is extremely difficult to submerge the head and upper part of the body.

Remember these two facts and you will soon lose that early fear of the water which is such a handicap in learning to swim. Now we may consider some further useful suggestions for the pool or sea.

Confidence Practice No. 2—Walking and Balancing

As soon as possible, you must learn to walk in the water, for until you are used to it you will find it difficult, especially in moving water like the sea, to keep your balance when your body is more than half submerged. Whether in the swimming pool or in the sea, you will find the following practices a great help:

(a) Walk out to arm-pit depth, at first holding on to the hand-rail or scum-trough if in a pool, and then let go of your hold and practise walking slowly by sliding your feet along the bottom. You will discover that by walking more or less flat-footed your balance is easier to maintain.

(b) Next try to increase your speed of walking by using your arms, at first like a pair of oars moving both together, and later, like the crawl swimmer, by pulling with left and right arm and hand alternately. It is a good thing, incidentally, when you are practising these movements, to lower your shoulders in the water by leaning your body slightly forward from the waist, if necessary by bending your knees a little.

(c) Finally, try balancing like a stork on one leg.

Confidence Practice No. 3—Giant Strides

This follows easily from the last practice, although for it you require a helper or a float of some kind. The helper is probably better because, as mentioned earlier in this book, under certain circumstances the use of a float by a non-swimmer may prove dangerous. Stand in the water up to the waist level, stretch your arms forward, and grasp the waist of your partner, who should be facing the same way as you are. Your partner then walks forward and partly drags you along after him while you, by taking the biggest possible strides—or rather leaps—try to throw each leg alternately up to the surface. Note that your partner should try to get through the water as quickly as possible, and for this reason should use his arms to assist his progress, as in Confidence Practice No. 2 (b). You will see what is meant if you study the following diagrams for a moment.

In diagram 3b you will see that if your partner walks fast enough, there will be times when both your feet will be off the bottom, with your body more or less trailing behind.

Confidence Practice No. 4—The Crouching Float

Walk out again until the water reaches armpit level, get your balance, reach forward with your arms, take a deep breath, and submerge your face and shoulders, as in diagram 4a. Now slowly raise your knees up to your chest and hold your crouching position until your breath begins to give out, 4b, then return slowly to standing again.

3a

3b

You may, if you wish, arrange for someone to assist you in your early efforts at this last practice by holding

4*a*   4*b*

your hands. If you do, tell your friend not to give you any support by lifting, but merely to keep you steady at the end of your practice when you attempt to regain your feet. You will notice, as you did when in the bath at home, how extremely buoyant the water is, especially if it is salt water.

Confidence Practice No. 5—Gliding and Regaining the Standing Position

Stand in the water up to waist level, with your back to the bath wall. Your partner should be facing you, about four yards to your front, with his shoulders under water and arms stretched forward under water towards you, palms facing upwards. Now stretch your arms forward, palms downwards, and submerge your shoulders under the water; lift one leg back and place your foot on the wall behind you. You are now ready to glide across the water, the foundation on which all swimming strokes are built.

Take and hold a deep breath and at the same time lower your face in the water and push towards your partner's hands by pressing hard on the wall with the raised foot and lifting up the other leg. Both legs should end up straight and together behind you, with the body stretched out on top of the water. Look at the two diagrams below:

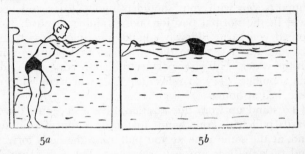

5a   5b

When you feel your partner's hands under yours, press down on his hands, at the same time lifting your head backwards and tucking your knees up under your chest. This will cause your hips to sink and you will end sitting up in the water with your feet pointing down to the bottom of the bath. Keep your shoulders under the water and push your feet down; then, when your feet are safely on the bottom, just stand up.

After a few more attempts, repeat the exercise, but this time press down on the water instead of on your partner's hands; you will find that you will be able to stand up just as easily. Your partner should be standing by at first, just in case you need him. Once you have mastered this exercise and can get back on to your feet without splashing and stumbling about, see how far you can glide before you have to stand up.

Confidence Practice No. 6—Regaining Feet from Back Floating

You need the help of your partner once again for your first few attempts. Stand in the water up to waist level, with your partner standing behind you. Submerge your shoulders and lean backwards, with your partner supporting you under the shoulders. It is important that he does not try to hold you out of the water, but merely supports you with your shoulders under water and head held in the normal position, not straining forward. Now spread your arms sideways, hands just under water, and let your legs rise up to the surface so that you are lying on the water, with your partner still supporting you under the shoulders. Try to relax just as if you were lying on your bed at home.

To stand up from this position, give a sweeping downwards pull with your hands in the direction of your feet and, at the same time as you pull, raise the head forward and tuck the legs up on to the chest. This will cause the hips to sink and you are in the same position, sitting in the water, as in the previous exercise; all you do now is to stand up in the same way. When you feel confident, try without the assistance of your partner.

Confidence Practice No. 7—Back Floating with Feet under Rail

Try to obtain the assistance of a friend for this practice, which is simply that of fixing the feet under the rail and slowly stretching the body and legs until the horizontal position is reached. Ask your partner to stand behind you and, for your first two or three attempts, to hold your head in his hands to make sure it does not go under. If you carry out this movement very slowly, you will find it possible to keep your face above water the whole of the time, even although your partner may be no longer assisting you.

Confidence Practice No. 8—Sculling Practice

It is best to try this practice first at home, in order to get an idea of the movement. Lie on your back on the floor, with your legs together and arms at the sides of your body. Now place the palms of your hands flat on the floor. This is the starting position. To begin the sculling movement, you turn your hands palm outwards and slide them away from your body for a distance of about twelve inches, keeping the thumb sides of your hands in contact with the floor. Now close your arms to your body again, turning your hands palm inwards and sliding them on the floor, the little finger side in contact. Repeat this 'out-and-in' movement continuously with a full wrist movement, and after a few times allow your elbows to bend slightly on the outward movement. You have already learned how to hold your back-floating position with feet fixed under the rail. You now take up this position again and, when fully stretched out, you begin your sculling practice, counting mentally, 'out, in, out, in,' to a time approximating brisk walking. Two injunctions will help you to carry out the movement correctly: firstly, 'push the water towards your feet,' and secondly, 'press down on the water.' When you feel that you have gained sufficient confidence to have a go away from the rail, give a slight push-off from the side of the bath with your toes and continue the sculling movement with your hands and arms; but have your friend standing by for your initial efforts.

Confidence Practice No. 9—Jumping In

You will probably have carried out all the foregoing practices after wading to the required depth. Next, if you have access to a swimming bath, you may go a stage further in your confidence training and practise jumping in from the side. Take up a standing position on the edge of the bath on a level with a depth of between waist and armpits. Bend down to a crouching position, and grasp the side of the bath, or, if possible, the hand-rail, with one hand, then jump in with a turn to face the side of the bath and grasp with both hands as you enter the water. After a few of these practices you should be ready to have a go at jumping in without grasping the rail for support. Yet it is a good thing not to be in too much of a hurry to attempt this latter stage, unless you can arrange for a friend to stand in the water and assist you to your feet for your first few jumps. Once you can jump in, you will never want to go down the steps again.

Miscellaneous Confidence Practices

Besides those already mentioned, there are many games and activities which could be included in a list of confidence practices. Activities like 'Leap frog in the Water' and simple games with a ball such as 'Intercepting in Threes' or 'Pig in the Middle' are obvious examples. Those which have been chosen above, however, are of a type which serve the double purpose of helping the learner to become used to the water on the one hand and of preparing the way for the practice of definite swimming skills on the other. That is to say, they are not only confidence practices but also preparatory exercises. You will naturally wish to play about in the water, especially if you are very young; but let me give you some advice on this point. Do not waste too much time on play, and, unless you have plenty of room such as in the sea, do not play games which are likely to interfere with the more serious efforts or enjoyment of others.

CHAPTER IV

The Breast Stroke

If your learning is to take place in a swimming bath and not in the sea, and if, as occasion requires, you are able to obtain the assistance of a friend for some of the practices, it is probably best for you to start your actual swimming lessons on the Breast Stroke. If, on the other hand, you are learning in the sea—and entirely on your own—my advice to you is that you should defer practice on the breast stroke until you have more or less mastered the Front Crawl. In either case, read through the paragraph on gliding in Chapter III and practise it carefully, as this is the foundation on which both strokes are built.

A Plan of Study and Practice

We shall proceed with the study and practice of the breast stroke as we intend to continue throughout the entire course of training. First of all, we will try to obtain a general 'mind picture' of the complete stroke, and then, by analysing or splitting it up into its component parts, we will make ourselves thoroughly familiar with the details. Finally, after practising each part separately, we will piece them together, stage by stage, until we have reconstructed the picture in actual movement.

General Description of the Breast Stroke

The best way to obtain a true 'mind picture' of any swimming stroke is to observe a really good swimmer performing in the water. Failing this, a useful alternative is to obtain your picture from watching a suitable film. There are some good 16 mm. Swimming Films available, and most communities nowadays have access to a projector. Whatever means you may use to develop your mind picture, do the job thoroughly. For example, observe closely such things as timing, breathing and the general poise of the body.

We must not go too fast, however, for some of you will be depending on a 'word picture' for your image. So let us try to explain what the breast stroke looks like and add a diagram or two where necessary. Briefly, the breast stroke consists of four main parts:

1   The Leg Thrust, or Kick, followed by
2   The Glide, followed by
3   The Arm Pull, followed by
4   The Combined Recovery of Arms and Legs.

Now study the following diagrams:

There are two sources of propulsion—the *Leg Thrust* and the *Arm Pull*. These two forces are applied separately and in such a way that when the actual thrust or pull occurs, the rest of the body is more or less streamlined. This fact is very important and will repay a closer study. Look again at diagram 6b which shows the leg thrust, or rather that part of it in which the legs are thrust astride and are now beginning to close like a pair of scissors. Note what has happened to the arms; they are now stretched forward while the leg thrust occurs so as to streamline the forward end of the body and consequently enable the force of the leg thrust to be utilised to the best advantage.

The leg thrust ends when the legs are closed, and now comes the *Glide*. This is a very important part of the stroke which, when well performed, is the hallmark of the good breast stroke swimmer. In the glide, the whole body is fully stretched, arms forward, legs backward with toes stretched backward so that the soles of the feet are showing just below the surface of the water. A good swimmer will glide as much as three yards after his leg thrust and *could* cover the entire length of a hundred feet swimming bath in as few as five or six strokes. It is during this glide that the swimmer exhales, blowing out through his mouth and nostrils with his face submerged.

The Arm Pull

When the glide is beginning to lose its momentum, the arms add their quota to the task of propelling the body forward; and while they are contributing their bit, it is clear to see that the best position for the legs is—yes, of course! —together, that is, streamlined. By this time you should be beginning to appreciate the stroke. Look at the previous diagrams once again. *The leg thrust drives the body forward into its glide*, the arms then take up the work and pull, and while they are pulling, the legs accommodate themselves to the job in hand and keep out of the way. Now comes

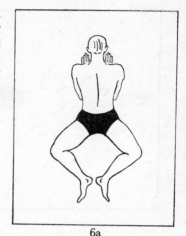

6a

6b

6c

6d

The Combined Recovery of Arms and Legs

You will understand that in the recovery, which is **a**
necessary preparation for the next stroke, or cycle of

movements, the action of both arms and legs is retarding the swimmer's progress. For this reason it is important that recovery should not be too vigorous, nor should it occupy too long a time. Look at diagram 6a again. The arms have finished their pull and are now tucked in close to the body in preparation for the next stretch forward which accompanies the leg thrust. We will consider the exact detail of this and all other parts of the stroke when we come to the next section of our study which deals with analysis. While the arms are being tucked away, the legs, you will notice, are being recovered in readiness for their thrust, the knees being bent outwards. In that way, they are kept as near to the surface of the water as possible, the heels touching each other and the toes turned out.

Breathing

In the breast stroke, the breath is inhaled as the arms make their pull, the head being lifted to bring the mouth clear of the surface. The breath is then exhaled during the leg thrust and glide. Remember our previous generalisation— breathe in through the mouth and out through nose and mouth.

Stroke Analysis and Practices: The Front Glide

This is the most important part of the stroke, so we will consider it first. A good deal of preparation can be carried out at home. Lie face downwards on the floor with arms stretched forward, thumbs interlocked, palm of the hands down, legs fully stretched, knees and ankles pressed together, and toes stretched back along the floor. Now drop your head until your chin and the tip of your nose rest lightly on the floor. In this position, although your head is not quite as low as it should be, you are as near to the gliding position as is possible on land.

Home Practices for the Breast Stroke

You will find that by studying carefully the following Home Practices in 'Land Drills' and practising them assiduously, you will not only reduce considerably the time spent on your water practices but you will also gain a much firmer knowledge of the actual details of the movement.

1 *The Arm Pull*

After the glide there comes the 'Pull,' and we should remind ourselves that the arm pull is unaccompanied by any other movement. By that I mean that while the arms make their pull, the legs should be held in a fully stretched position, that is, streamlined. Lie down prone on the bed—*across* the bed preferably so as not to be hampered by pillows or the bed ends—and adjust yourself so that your head and shoulders are hanging over the side. Pull, by pressing downwards and sideways, with the hands and arms. Remember to keep the arms straight, as in Diagrams 7a and 7b. The hands can be either straight or slightly cupped.

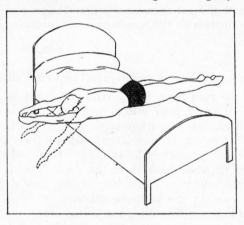

7a

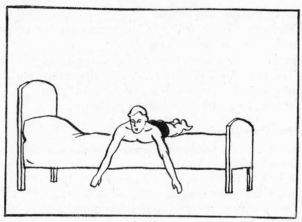

7b

Note carefully that at the end of the pull, the hands are about 12 inches lower than they were at the beginning. The arms, when viewed from the front, make an angle of about 90°. Throughout the pull, the hands and elbows should be in front of the shoulders. If you can see your hands out of the corners of your eyes, without moving your head, then they will be in the correct position. But if you lose sight of your hands at any time, then you are pulling them too far back. The arm pull serves two purposes:

(*a*) By pressing downwards, it provides the necessary power for lifting the head to breathe in.

(*b*) By pressing sideways as well as downwards it provides a certain amount of propulsion, which is needed to offset the retarding action of bending the knees for the leg drive.

It is important to remember that if you do pull your arms beyond the shoulder line, the following faults will occur:

(*a*) Body balance will be lost.
(*b*) The arms will be pulling the body under water, instead of assisting in forward propulsion.
(*c*) It will make breathing extremely difficult.
(*d*) The retarding effect of recovering the arms from this position will greatly check your forward speed.
(*e*) It will throw the timing of the stroke out.

2 *The Arm Recovery*

As we have said before, the purpose of the arm recovery is to tuck the arms away in preparation for the next part of the stroke which, you will remember, is the glide. This recovery has to be done in such a way that the resistance to the swimmer's progress is at a minimum. The problem for us to solve, then, is how to move our arms from their position at the end of the pull to their position for the glide— that is, straight in front of the body—without applying the brakes. We would not, of course, keep the arms straight while carrying them forward, because the resistance would obviously cancel out the result of the pull.

We shall find that the best way to solve the problem is to push the elbows downwards towards the floor and bring them in under the shoulders. This action will bring the hands together just in front of the face, as in Diagram 8*b*.

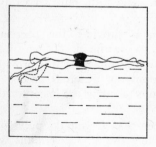

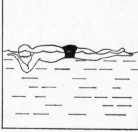

8*a*   8*b*

Notice that at no time in the recovery do the hands or elbows come beyond the line of the shoulders.

From this position the arms are now stretched forward into the glide. As this movement does not aid in propulsion, do not make it a vigorous action or hold the arms too tense. It should be a smooth, easy movement, giving the muscles a chance to relax, in readiness for the next pull.

3 Co-ordination of the Arm Movements

Having studied the arm movements—the pull and the recovery—separately, we will now string them together and observe how they make up the complete arm cycle and how they are related to the breathing. You will find it useful to practise the following exercise, first in the standing position and later in the prone position, and to continue the practice until you are able to perform it automatically without thinking about it.

Take up a comfortable stance with the feet either together or only slightly apart; then lean forward from the waist and bring the arms into the 'recovery' position, with the backs of the hands under your chin and your elbows under your shoulders. Now practise the arm cycle to the count of six in waltz time as follows:

(*a*) Stretch forward with arms and breathe out—Count 1, 2, 3.

(*b*) Make your arm pull and breathe in—Count 4, 5.

(*c*) Arm recovery—Count 6.

Remember to lock your thumbs together as you reach forward so as to avoid the common fault of shortening the glide by parting your arms too soon. This six-beat timing for the breast stroke is a new idea which is well worth adopting if you are really trying to teach yourself. Its advantage lies in the fact that waltz time is very easy to follow and suits the rhythm not only of the breast stroke but also, in fact, of all the swimming strokes. Try it again,

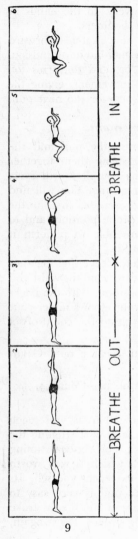

9

remembering that the first three beats are occupied by nothing more than the forward stretch of the arms and a pause while the arms are in position with hands together. Look at the accompanying strip diagram of the complete stroke in its six-beat time stages.

Keep on repeating this arm practice until you are confident of having mastered the timing, then adjust your breathing so as to exhale on beats 1, 2 and 3 and inhale on beats 4 and 5. Note that there are no jerky actions in swimming, so aim at a smooth co-ordination of all movements, making each one pass into the next without any sharp division or boundary.

If you are now satisfied that you know the arm movements of the breast stroke and have practised them, first standing, then in in a prone position over a padded chair, and lastly in time with breathing, we will next turn our attention to the leg movements.

Leg Movements of the Breast Stroke

Contrary to what is commonly believed, the main force of the breast stroke 'kick' does not come from the kick itself, that is the actual straightening of the legs from their position of recovery, but rather from the movement of the legs from the wide open to the closed position—the scissor movement. To elucidate this point, lie face down on the carpet or bed with your legs straight and as wide apart as possible. Now, without bending the knees, close the legs strongly together. Practise this as much as you can, because it is this closing movement which contributes most thrust when you are swimming. Bearing this in mind, let us study the leg movement in detail. Look at the following diagrams:

In diagram 10a, which illustrates the leg recovery, the knees are drawn up, not *under* the body but sideways. This is the first and most important point for you to learn. In 10b the legs are opened as wide as possible, and then they are closed to make a perfectly straight line, fully streamlined.

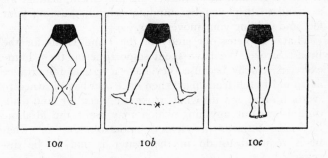

10a   10b   10c

Leg Practice No. 1

Sit on the floor with your legs stretched out in front of you and with your arms propping up your body. Now bend your knees outwards while keeping your heels together, with toes turned out. From this sitting position stretch your legs widely astride and, without pausing,

C*

close them firmly together. This practice should give you a good idea of the leg recovery and the kick or 'thrust.' You may try bending you knees outwards while you are lying in the prone position, but although that will give you a better idea of the actual movement, you will find it impossible—unless you are unusually supple—to perform such an action with both legs simultaneously.

Leg Practice No. 2

Lie across a padded chair or, if one is available, a large pouffe. Rest your hands on the floor and stretch your legs backwards, keeping them together, feet and ankles touching, toes stretched backwards. Lie on your abdomen so as to leave your legs free to move. From this position, bend your knees, keeping them as high off the floor as possible, heels touching each other, toes turned outwards. Now kick wide sideways, and without a pause close the legs together. If you find it difficult to master this movement, arrange for a friend to help you by standing behind, grasping your feet and guiding your movements.

That completes our study of the Land Drills for the Breast Stroke. We have spent some time on these home exercises, chiefly because they have a special importance as an aid to self-teaching. When once you have learned to swim, no matter with what stroke, the need for land drills diminishes, but anything which may assist the absolute beginner towards a clearer understanding of what he is required to do in the water is not to be disregarded.

Breast Stroke: Water Practices

Let us assume that the learner is now ready for his first real lesson in the water. He has already gained a certain degree of confidence through the practice of the special water skills outlined in the previous chapter, and he has studied and practised the exercises prescribed for home preparation. The following rules for water practice will be found useful if applied:

Rule 1

Before each visit to the baths, make sure that you have carried out and understood your home preparation or at least those portions of it which are relevant to the work about to be done in the water.

Rule 2

Plan every lesson and stick to your practice schedule.

Rule 3

When you have finished a water session, take stock of what you have achieved and make a note of anything which you have left uncompleted.

The following list of water practices should be followed methodically, each new skill being tackled with the will to continue its practice until achievement results.

1 Gliding Practice

You cannot do too much of this excellent preparatory exercise, so every time that you visit the swimming baths make a point of including a few glides in your practice schedule. You may remember that we dealt with the details of gliding in Chapter III.

2 Leg Practices at the Rail

The assistance of a helper is most valuable for this practice, at any rate during the early stages. The first thing to learn is how to grasp the rail, for although the precise grasp does not really matter when a partner is at hand to support your legs, it is essential to use the correct method when you are on your own.

Proceed into fairly deep water and take an undergrip on the rail, that is, place your hands under the rail with your palms upwards, and then grasp from below. Now raise first one leg and then the other for your partner to support. Tell him to grasp your feet, with his thumbs over the middle of the soles, so that his fingers are round your instep. Fix your elbows against the side of the bath directly below your hands, which should be about shoulder-width apart. This position should look something like this:

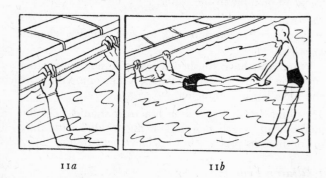

11a   11b

This is the starting position for your leg practices, which should be done slowly at first, with your partner supporting and guiding your feet. With your legs fully stretched behind, feet and ankles touching each other, toes stretched so that, the soles of your feet are close to the surface of the water, you begin your practice as soon as you are both ready.

(a) *Leg Recovery*

Bend your knees outwards, remembering your land drills. Your partner can assist by exerting some slight leverage on your feet which will tend to keep your knees up. Remember that in this leg recovery, your heels should be touching each other and your feet turned outwards.

(b) *Leg Thrust*

Stretch your legs wide sideways and then, without pausing, close them together. Your partner should make sure that your kick is wide and that the scissor movement, when you close your legs, is firm. At the end of the stroke, pause for a second or two before you make your next recovery.

(c) Repetition

Make use of your partner only so long as is necessary for you to master the actual form or path of the movement. He will soon know by your efforts to follow his guiding hands when to let go of your feet and leave you to your own resources. When he does release you, you will find that your legs will begin to sink, and this is where you will discover the advantage of the undergrip on the rail, because by using your forearms as levers—by pressing them against the bath side with your elbows—you can lever yourself into the horizontal position and maintain it without much effort.

(d) Leg Stroke Timing

Remembering your six-beat timing, you might, after making sure that you have learned the movement, perform it to the count of six as follows: bend the legs on counts 5 and 6, stretch and close them on count 1, and hold them together for 2, 3 and 4 (the glide). It may help you to run over this counting in your mind a few times—'Kick, two, three, four—and—bend; kick, two, three, four—and—bend; kick . . .' and so on.

3 Leg Practice with a Partner Moving

This next practice gives you a much better idea of the leg stroke because you are moving through the water. There are several methods of obtaining assistance for this, but the best one is probably to stand in water up to your armpit level, face your partner and rest your hands on his shoulders. Then tell him to place his hands, fingers pointing downwards, on the lower part of your chest, as in sketch 12a. Next, with his assistance, raise your legs behind you into position (*b*) and then start your leg stroke, while your partner walks backwards. The position of his hands when you are in the horizontal is as if he were carrying a tray.

12*a*   12*b*

A very common fault associated with this practice is that the performer tries to lift his head too high out of the water. Sometimes, indeed, he tries to lift his shoulders out, too. So remember the rule—'keep you chin in the water'.

4 Leg Practice with a Float

If you have made good progress at the previous exercises, you may now try to get along on your own. Any float will do—an inflated ring, an airtight can, or a slab of cork. The cork float is probably the best, because its proper use enables the learner to keep on an even keel. Whichever aid you decide to use, start with a glide from a push-off from the side of the bath, and keep your arms fully stretched in front of you. Shoulders and chin should be in the water all the time. One word of warning is necessary—whatever happens, do not swim out of your depth, even though you may feel quite confident with your float.

Breast Stroke—Arm Practices in the Water

You will already have done much of the arm work for the breast stroke at home; but there is a big difference between land and water practices, even though in appearance the movements are precisely the same. So far, no mention has been made of the work that is done by the *hand* in swimming, and of the importance of using it in the correct manner. It was once considered that a tightly-cupped hand with thumb and finger held close together was absolutely essential to good swimming, but more recently, since it has been observed that a great many first-class swimmers habitually swim with a relaxed hand—that is, with little or no attempt to keep the fingers or the thumb closed—many coaches are discounting the old rule. In this connection it would probably be wise to advise the learner to keep the hands *loosely cupped*, and if there should be a slight gap between the fingers, do not trouble to check it.

Arm Practice (i)—Leaning against the Wall of the Bath

Stand with feet astride about 18 inches from the wall of the bath and then lean backwards to rest your hips against the wall, with your arms in the 'recovery' position. Remembering your home preparation, practise the co-ordinated arm movements to the six-beat count. Stretch the arms forward on 1 and hold them forward on 2 and 3, pull on 4, and recover on 5 and 6. If, while doing this continuously, you say to yourself mentally—'kick—two—three—pull—two—three', it will assist you to visualise the combined arm and leg movements.

Remember that the direction of the pull is downwards

as well as outwards and that the hands, which in the forward position are only just below the surface, should be about one foot deep at the end of the pull. After a few minutes' work on this practice, add the correct breathing—'out' on 1, 2, and 3 with face submerged, and 'in' on 4 and 5 with the head lifted. You will have noticed that leaning back against the wall counteracts your arm pull and keeps you anchored.

Arm Practice (ii)—From the Glide

Push off in a glide from the side of the bath and after a short glide with face submerged while breathing out, make your arm pull, breathe in, arm recovery, and forward stretch again. In other words insert an arm co-ordination into the glide. You can, in fact, learn to swim from this stage of your instruction simply by building on the foundation work of the glide, adding bit by bit as follows:

Stage 1—The Glide.

Stage 2—The Glide and Pull.

Stage 3—The Glide, Pull, Recover Arm and Legs.

Stage 4—The Glide, Pull, Recover Arms and Legs, and then Glide again.

Arm Practice (iii)—Partner Assisting

While Practice (ii) enables the learner to conceive the arm movements in relation to the rest of the stroke the effort required for gliding makes it impossible for him to maintain the practice for long. It is a good thing, then, to ask a partner to assist you into a front gliding position. To do that, he should stand at the side of you, facing your head and grasping your sides as you lie out on the water. As your perform your arm movements with correct breathing, he walks beside you and gives you just that little bit of help necessary to prevent your legs from sinking. It would be an advantage if he would help you further by counting 'kick—two—three—pull—two—three' to indicate the timing and to remind you of where the kick would come in the completed stroke. This practice should be continued until its co-ordination becomes automatic, that is, until you can perform it without the slightest concentration on the work in hand.

If you are using inflatable armbands, as previously described in Chapter I, you may be able to do this and some of the following practices without the assistance of a partner.

Combined Practices for Arms and Legs

Here again you need the services of a helper, and the method of assisting can be either that explained in the last practice or, if you are in deeper water, for your partner to hold you up as he might hold a tray—on both arms held forward.

(a) Combined Practice—Stationary

Adopt the front floating position and work through the movements slowly at first. Remember the sequence—(1) The Arm Pull (legs together); (2) The Recovery (arms and legs); (3) The Leg Thrust (arms forward). Repeat these movements over and over until you can perform them in good time, and ask your partner to count for you—'kick, two, three; pull, two, three'.

(b) Combined Practice—Moving

This is a simple progression on the foregoing exercise which, however, makes it necessary for your helper to adopt either the earlier method of support—that is, from above—or, if you have sufficient confidence in him, another method in which, in deep water, he supports you from underneath with one hand only. This leaves his other hand free to help him to keep up with you.

Here are one or two final words of advice which cannot be reiterated too often:

1 Do not prolong your arm pull beyond the line of your shoulders, that is to say, beyond a line running perpendicularly from your shoulder tip.

2 Keep your eyes just above surface level when gliding.

3 Breathe in through the mouth and out through the nose and mouth.

4 Do not hurry your glide.

First Attempts by Yourself

Now for the great adventure. If you have studied and practised carefully and adequately, you should not find it difficult to achieve your aim of swimming without assistance, if only for a stroke or two. One of the best methods for this first attempt is to get a friend to give you some light support for a few strokes and then gradually to withdraw his assistance and so leave you on your own. The advantage of this method is that the beginner knows that if he should get into any difficulties there is someone at hand to help him to his feet; consequently, he may set about his 'first solo' with greater confidence. Another method is to stand about three yards from the hand-rail and glide and swim to it, increasing the distance as you improve. Finally there is the method mentioned earlier—building up the stroke from the push-off and glide from the side of the bath. Whichever method you do adopt, good luck to you at this thrilling moment!

CHAPTER V

The Crawl

Sooner or later, everyone who desires to become a swimmer aspires to swim the crawl. It is customary nowadays to dispense with the term 'Front Crawl,' the two crawl strokes now being called 'The Crawl' and 'The Back Crawl'. Its popularity is, of course, justified, for it is the fastest of all known strokes, it is probably the most natural of all strokes, it is certainly a real delight to perform well, and it is easily adaptable to individual differences of age and strength. Furthermore, it can be modified for the purpose of swimming the Channel or for winning a one-length sprint.

Description of the Stroke

Unlike the Breast and old style Back Strokes, whose movements are symmetrical, those of the Crawl are to a certain extent asymmetrical. That is to say, the arms are moved one at a time to produce the pull, while the legs are moved up and down alternately. The number of leg movements or beats to each complete arm cycle—left and right—depends on the build of the swimmer and the purpose of the stroke. Thus for fast swimming, a small man or woman may adopt a six-beat or even an eight-beat leg action, while for long distance swimming a four-beat crawl is frequently employed. An important point to remember is that there are, in fact, two distinct styles of crawl swimming which may be used by the same swimmer on different occasions.

In really fast swimming, it is possible, by raising the

head and shoulders and by arching the back, to give effect to the hydroplane principle, by which the upper part of the body skims or planes over the surface of the water instead of ploughing through it. The result, of course, is a much lessened resistance to progress, and consequently more speed. If, however, you attempted to raise your head and shoulders out of the water when swimming *slowly*, your legs would sink low and cause an inevitable drag.

The fact that the front crawl is so much faster than, for example, the breast stroke, is due to three factors. One is the lifting of the arms out of the water during their recovery. Another is the timing of the propelling forces which, following each other in smooth and continuous rhythm, sustain an even momentum uninterrupted by drag. The third factor is that the legs, in moving up and down, more or less without pause, are continuously propelling the body forward.

Initial Stroke—Breast or Crawl?

Many experts maintain that one should begin one's swimming education by first learning the crawl. Others are equally emphatic as to the advantages of first learning the breast stroke. A few of our best coaches hold the view that it matters little or not at all which stroke you start with, so long as you know what you are doing and so long as you persevere with one stroke until you reach a fairly good standard of performance before you attempt the next stroke. One or two observations may help you to decide.

The chief advantages of the breast stroke as the initial one for the learner are:

1 Its mechanics are probably more easily understood by the beginner, who, in consequence, finds it easier to analyse and build up by stages.

2 It can be learnt without having to submerge the face and so it will be preferred by the timid person who not

only finds it very difficult to breathe out under water but also likes to see where he is going.

3 Once the breast stroke has been mastered, a swimmer finds it very easy to modify it for treading water, that is, for resting purposes.

The main advantages of beginning with the crawl stroke are:

1 It is probably slightly less difficult to learn if undertaken in the right way.

2 It is more satisfying to the majority of performers who prefer a speedy stroke.

3 Its basic movements and timing are closely related to those of the back crawl, and because of this it serves as a useful stepping stone to this latter stroke.

On the whole, therefore, it is largely a matter of individual choice, and if one were asked for advice, the best answer would be—choose the stroke you can understand *easier* and work first on that one. There is one point, however, in favour of the crawl when special facilities are available. If, for example, the learner has access to shallow water such as is sometimes possible in a bath specially designed for learners, or at the seaside where one may find shallow lagoons left by the tide, there is little doubt that the crawl is the easier stroke to learn. We will consider this method— the shallow water one—in detail at a later stage. In the meantime, let us study the crawl stroke more closely, so as to obtain as complete a picture as possible to assist us in our practices.

Position of Body

The general position of the body is horizontal, the head being held in such a position that the swimmer, when on an even keel, cuts the water with his forehead, his eyes being just below or just above the surface. It is important to remember, however, that for fast swimming the head is raised higher and the back arched to give effect to the hydroplaning principle.

Body Roll

As each arm is lifted from the water at the end of its pull, the body is rolled slightly over to counterbalance the weight, and to enable the hand and arm to be lifted clear. It is a common mistake to roll more than is absolutely necessary, and in fast swimming, because the shoulders are raised higher out of the water, the roll should be almost imperceptible.

Breathing

Although it is usual for some swimmers when sprinting to hold their breath for several strokes, it is best to learn to breathe in and out with each complete cycle of the arms, that is to say, breathe in as you recover one arm from the water and out as you recover the other. By turning your head sideways and by tucking your chin close in to your shoulders, you can breathe in through your mouth without having to roll more than is absolutely necessary. Breathing out begins as soon as you have finished inhaling and is effected through the nose and mouth while the face is submerged.

The Arm Action of the Crawl

(a) The Entry

The hand enters the water in front of the head on a line continuous with the long axis of the body or, in other words, in front of the centre line of the forehead. As the hand enters the water, the elbow is raised rather higher so as to be carried clear of the surface, thereby avoiding drag. This turns the forearm and hand so that the thumb side of the hand enters first, with the palm of the hand turned outwards. As the hand takes hold of the water, it is turned palm downwards, due partly to the roll of the body on to an 'even keel' and partly to the straightening of the elbow. The arm drives forward and downward, the forearm, as it were, following the path of the hand to avoid splash. As soon as the arm is submerged, and without any pause whatsoever, the arm takes up and starts it next phase, which is—

(b) The Arm Pull

At first, the pressure of the hand on the water is in a downward direction, again following the line of the centre of the body. The movement of the arm continues until the hand has traced a rough semi-circle, starting with the 'catch' and ending when the thumb reaches the side of the thigh. During the pull, the arm is almost, but not quite, straightened; there are three reasons for this. One is to lessen the strain on the arm which a longer lever would cause; another is to keep the hand travelling along the centre line and thus to prevent roll; and the third reason—a very important one—is to prevent over-reaching, which lessens the power of the pull and throws the body out of its course. Diagram 13 illustrates the advantages of the bent arm pull.

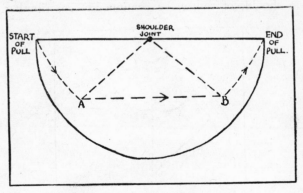

13

The dotted lines represent the direction of the hand when the pull is made with a *bent* arm, while the continuous line represents the path of the hand in a *straight arm* pull. You will see that with the bent arm pull, the first phase (to position A) is in a downward and backward direction and consequently is not contributing much to the swimmer's progress. But from position A to position B, because of the bent arm, the hand is able to apply its maximum power by pulling horizontally backward over a considerable distance. Because the main force of the pull is applied in this way—parallel with the long axis of the swimmer's body—it secures much more driving power than would be obtained from a straight arm, whose curve shows that throughout the whole pull the hand is moving either downward and backward or upward and backward, consequently causing much dissipation of effort.

This next sketch shows the direction of the arm pull when viewed from the front. It should be noted that the hand travels along a line parallel to the long axis of the body.

From the time the hand enters the water until it brushes the side of the thigh at the end of the pull, the hand and arm should, of course, be continuously contributing to

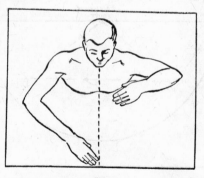

14

the task of propelling the body through the water, just as the blade of an oar exerts pressure on the water throughout the 'pull.' You will appreciate, however, that the most important part of the arm pull occurs in the middle third of the stroke as the arm approaches and passes its vertical position below the shoulder.

(c) The Arm Recovery

Having made its pull, with the hand continuing its work until it reaches the thigh, the arm is lifted quickly out of the water with just that amount of body turn or roll as is necessary to enable it to be carried upwards and forwards for the next entry. In order to avoid drag, the elbow should be drawn out first, the forearm and hand following the same path. With the elbow up, the arm is swung or thrown forward, the hand being kept just clear of the surface and the wrist and fingers being fully relaxed. This recovery is performed quickly, much more quickly in fact than the pull. The reason for this is that if the action were performed slowly, the body would have to roll more deeply to counteract the weight of the arm. So remember that a quick arm recovery reduces body roll.

Now because the recovery is quick and the pull comparatively slow, a time gap (which must be filled in) is inevitably caused. The best position for the arm while waiting for its fellow to finish its pull is in front of the head and just under the water, where, after the entry of the hand, it may be allowed to rest or glide. It should be mentioned, however, that in very fast crawl swimming, this arm glide is almost imperceptible.

The Leg Action of the Crawl

The general appearance of the legs of a good crawl swimmer is that of two flails working in opposition. The feet make little or no splash, the heels merely breaking the surface, and the ankles and feet are fully stretched all

the time, the soles of the feet being visible at the top of
each thrash or beat. The action takes place as follows:

From a relaxed position with the leg riding on the surface
of the water, the knee is lowered by a movement at the
hip joint corresponding to the action of the thigh in walking
a step forward. In walking, this action would cause the
leg to swing forward to the point where the heel meets
the ground, but in the water, because of the greater
resistance, the leg and foot tend to drag. When the knee
has dropped about 18 inches, the thigh is then forced
upwards vigorously; and because the leg and foot are
relaxed, this causes a whip-like or flail-like action, which
locks the knee and returns the whole leg to the
surface.

As one leg goes down, of course, the other comes up, and
in order to obtain the maximum effect from their combined action, the toes must be turned inwards slightly,
and toes and knees should almost touch their fellows as
they pass. Experts differ as to how deep the leg should
be allowed to travel, but as this depends on the speed of
the movement and on whether the swimmer is tall or
short, we may take it that the average depth is about
18–20 inches. It is important always to bear in mind that
it is the *upthrust* and not the downthrust which gives you
the drive.

Timing

For all ordinary purposes, six leg beats to one complete
arm cycle is generally agreed to be the best. This number,
however, can be modified to four for leisurely swimming
or to eight for speed swimming if one is small and nimble
of physique.

Breathing

The crawl swimmer breathes in and out with every complete stroke. You should inhale through the mouth as

you lift one arm from the water, turning your head towards your shoulder and resting the side of your face in the water. This is not so difficult as it may seem at first because your head, as you are swimming, makes a kind of bow-wave which leaves a trough just where your mouth is. You exhale with your face submerged as you roll on to an even keel to make your next entry. There are one or two good coaches who recommend bilateral breathing—that is, breathing in on each side alternately. This method, it is claimed, corrects the tendency to deviate from the swimming line by maintaining an even balance. It is rather complicated, however, and might well be ignored by the learner until he has acquired a good grounding in the more fundamental techniques of the sport.

Home Preparation for the Crawl

Unlike the breast stroke, much of which can be learned on land, the crawl is best suited for water practice, even in its most elementary stages of learning. There are, however, one or two useful movements which it will pay the beginner to practise, if only for the purpose of giving him a better understanding of the water exercises.

1 The Arm Pull

If the learner lies full length along a narrow horizontal and raised plank, or on the edge of a bed or long table, he will find it useful to practise the three parts of the arm movement—the entry, the pull, and the recovery. It is important, however, that he should be able to move his arm freely underneath this plank or other support, in order to follow the correct line of pull as previously described. With a raised plank, of course, he can practise the combined arm movements, but on a wider support like a bed or table, his practice will be restricted to one arm at a time.

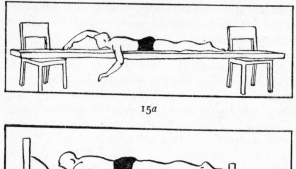

15*a*

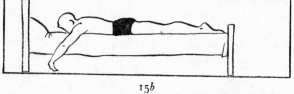

15*b*

2 *The Leg Thrash*

(*a*) Stand with your side against a wall and with one
hand resting against it for support. Now raise one knee
forward about 18–20 inches, allowing the leg and foot
to hang down fully relaxed from the knee. Now pull or
force the knee quickly backwards; this action will cause
a vigorous straightening of the knee. Finally, close the
legs to the original position. You will see by this simple
experiment what is meant by the whip or flail-like action
mentioned previously and you will also get the idea of the
strong upward drive which will be required when you pass
on to your water lessons.

(*b*) If you can find something from which to hang,
such as a bar or a conveniently situated branch of a tree,
you can try the leg thrash, working both legs in opposition.
Note that the action is very similar to walking, except for
the vigorous flick back of the lower leg. Note also that in
the hanging position you will be able to keep your toes
pointed downwards towards the ground and turned slightly

inwards, which is the correct relative position when actually swimming.

Apart from these two practices, there is little one can do at home which cannot be done better in the water. So let us now turn our attention to the water practices.

Front Crawl Water Practices

A The Shallow Water Method

If you have access to a shallow water learners' bath, or any piece of water of an even depth of 18–20 inches, your best way to learn the crawl is as follows. This method, by the way, is the ideal one for the very young child.

Practice (i)

Crawling on the hands with legs trailing behind. In shallow water, it is a fairly simple matter to walk or crawl on the hands with the legs stretched back horizontally, the mouth being held just above the water line so that breathing is not interfered with. At first, the pupil will wish to have the palms of his hands on the bottom and will have some difficulty in keeping his feet off the bottom, too. Later, however, as his skill and confidence increase, he will find it quite easy to pull himself along on his fingertips and hold his legs up to the surface.

Practice (ii)

Crawling on the hands using the Crawl leg action. This follows easily from the foregoing practice, and needs little further explanation. It will probably be of some assistance to the learner, especially if he is very young, to have the help during the early stages of the practice of father or brother or friend to grasp his feet and guide them up and down through the correct leg action.

Practice (iii)

The Dog Paddle. The next easy progression is the dog paddle, which is merely a development of the previous movements of the arms in which the hands, instead of walking along the bottom, are gradually removed and used as paddles. If you try to run on your hands instead of walking on them, you will unconsciously change to the Dog Paddle. Stretch the arms forward alternately and, using the hands as paddles, press down on the water and then backward, just like the front legs of a dog, in fact.

The next stage of the shallow water method is the same as that which will be described for practice in a normal swimming bath. The pupil who has worked at this method is, therefore, recommended to pick up the following course at the dog paddle stage (number 4).

B Water Practice at the Swimming Bath

Leg Practice No. 1

At the Rail. Take hold of the rail as you did in the practice for the breast stroke, using an undergrip and pressing your elbows against the wall of the bath underneath. Lift up your legs and balance the body in a horizontal position. You will find it a great help if at first you have the assistance of a good swimmer to guide your feet in their up and down movements; he can also grip your feet at the instep and see to it that:

(*a*) your toes are kept in a backward pointing position and turned slightly inwards;

(*b*) your legs are not lowered more than 18 to 20 inches; and

(*c*) your knees and ankles are close together as they pass each other.

Leg Practice No. 2

From the Glide. For this practice, we will assume that the pupil has followed the course right through from the beginning and has mastered the skill of a front glide from a push-off from the bath side, as described in the chapter on the breast stroke. From the standing position in water at armpit level and with your back to the wall of the bath, give a little jump to place your feet just under the rail; push off immediately, keeping your arms stretched forward, with thumbs locked and palms directed forward and downward to act as a hydroplane. The moment you push off you should begin your leg thrashing, counting one to six in your mind to establish the timing.

Leg Practice No. 3

With a Float or Leg Board. If you are lucky enough to be able to borrow a cork slab or a leg board, use this as an aid to your practice. The cork slab is about 18 inches by 12 inches by 2 inches and is best for the beginner because of its additional buoyancy. The leg board is slightly longer, has little buoyancy, and can only be used by a swimmer who can maintain sufficient speed to utilise the hydroplaning principle. In either case, the float or board is held by the longer sides and tilted up in front at an angle of about 20 degrees.

Leg Practice No. 4

With Dog Paddle. We shall be joined here by those pupils who have been practising their leg action with the shallow water method. If you cannot already swim—that is, if your are beginning your swimming course with the crawl stroke—you will require some support for this practice. Arrange for a friend to assist in holding you up by grasping each side of your waist and walking alongside you as you swim. The action of the arms is very similar to that of the forelegs of a dog when swimming or a trotting horse with a high knee action. Keep your elbows bent and move the hands as paddles in a circular movement, catching at the water with a downward and backward pressure. You will soon find you can dispense with assistance, and when you can paddle about 25 yards on your own, pass on to the next practice. By the way, when you are using the dog paddle, you may keep your mouth above water the whole time.

When you have gained some degree of skill at the above practice, introduce breathing in time with your leg beats, lifting your head clear to breathe in on 1, 2 and 3, and sinking your face to breathe out on 4, 5 and 6.

All these practices are very important and even when they have been mastered they should be used repeatedly to give strength to your legs and to test your leg action. Even the best swimmers spend a lot of time at their leg practices.

Arm Practice No. 1

Standing. Stand in the water at waist level and lean forward to submerge your shoulders and to rest your chin in the water. Make sure of this last point, for if you allow your chin to leave the water, the entire practice will be rendered valueless. Try the movements with one arm first— it does not matter which you use.

The Entry—Reach forward with one arm and hold your hand in front of your head just above the water, palm outwards. If you have studied the description carefully, you will recall that at this point, when the hand is ready to make its entry, the arm is slightly bent at the elbow and the elbow itself is rather higher than the hand. Now make sure that the whole of the limb is as completely relaxed as possible, give a final check up on your position and make your entry by closing your fingers so as to make a paddle and by piercing the water at an angle of about 30 degrees, the forearm following the path of the hand, that is, as it were, entering the same hole. When the arm is almost straight, start

The Arm Pull—This, you will remember, follows the centre line of the body, first in a downward direction, then backward. See that the arm is slightly bent during the pull and that you maintain pressure with your hand and arm throughout the entire movement until the thumb reaches the outer side of the thigh. Remember also that the strongest part of the pull should be made where its effect is greatest, that is, during its middle third as the arm approaches and passes the vertical. Keep your eyes open all the time and watch your hand to see that it is travelling along its true course.

The Arm Recovery—Because you are standing in the water—and, therefore, not horizontal—your hand, when it reaches the thigh, will be much lower in the water than when you are swimming. So to obtain a true conception of the recovery, you must continue your pull past your thigh until the hand, palm upwards, reaches the surface of the water behind you. Look at these two sketches:

16a   16b

Now lift the elbow, drawing behind it first the forearm then the hand, at the same time making sure that it is a clean withdrawal and that you are not dragging the hand against resistance. In other words, remember that, as in the entry, the forearm and hand take the same path. Next, with the hand clear of the surface and the wrist bent, bring the elbow fairly sharply forward, allowing the forearm

D

and hand to hang limply. The back of the hand should be just clear of the surface as it swings forward for its next entry, and as it passes the face, its palm, if the wrist is properly relaxed, should be facing outwards. In other words, if you are looking sideways during the recovery—as you would be if inhaling—it is the back of the hand which you should see as it passes your face. Repeat all the foregoing with the other arm.

Arm Practice No. 2

Standing. Having followed instructions carefully and practised with one arm, try it now with two arms. Still standing, start as you did for the past practice, with one hand poised for entry, but this time carry the other arm back to its position at the end of the pull. Obviously if your left arm is forward as you make your entry with it, you will start the recovery with your right. Practise very slowly at first before you attempt the exercise at normal swimming speed.

Breathing—Now that you have your arms working in combination, it is time to introduce the following correct breathing technique. First make a decision as towards which side you will turn your head when inhaling; then take up a position with one arm forward and one backward in readiness to make entry or recovery as the case may be. Now turn your head towards the side of your backward arm and rest the side of your face in the water, your opened mouth just clear. From this position make your arm recovery and breathe *in*, continuing to do so until the arm recovery is complete. As this same arm enters the water for its pull, your head will have returned to its forward position where, with face submerged, you breathe *out* under water through nostrils and mouth. If, after several attempts at this, you feel that you are making only slight headway, try breathing on the other side; you may find it easier there.

Arm Practice No. 3

With Legs Supported. There are several methods of providing support for the legs while the swimmer is able to concentrate on his arm action; three of the best will now be described.

Method (i)—Using the Rail—In this method, one foot is hooked over the top of the rail, while the other is fixed against the wall of the bath about 15 inches below. It is a difficult and somewhat uncomfortable method, but it is one which is regularly used by many first-class swimmers.

Method (ii)—Manual Support—In this method, an assistant stands by the side of the pupil and, helping him into a horizontal position, embraces him around the knees. He—the helper—should stand well back so as not to prevent the pupil from making a correct recovery. It is quite unnecessary for the assistant to use a great deal of effort in this method; a certain amount of leverage is required, but not so much as will cause the pupil to have his head clear of the water.

Method (iii)—Belt and Rope—This is perhaps the best method. Again you need a helper. You fix round your waist a belt to which is attached a length of rope; the other end of this you pass to your partner, who stands out on the side of the bath. With his assistance, you adopt a front floating position, with your toes touching the side of the bath. By holding the rope taut, he fixes your position while you practise. If you wish, you can dispense with a belt by covering a loop in the end of the rope with a length of hosepipe.

As in the standing position, practise these arm movements first without paying attention to your breathing and later adding the correct breathing method. Keep up these practices of arms and legs until you are certain that they are as correct as you can make them. Then—and only then—you can turn to the combined arm and leg work.

Combined Arm and Leg Practices

At first, the best plan is to build up your stroke by practising short distances such as one width of the bath. Make each movement as slow and deliberate as possible and concentrate on one phase at a time, until each has been correctly mastered. Try to cultivate the six-beat crawl from the start, counting mentally three leg beats to each arm pull. Before your attempt to swim fast, learn the art of swimming easily and accurately. No one, in fact, should attempt the racing style until his muscles, limbs, and breathing mechanism have been well co-ordinated after long sustained practice of the basic movement. In fact, all young swimmers are strongly advised to learn first to swim a mile with an easy crawl before trying to change their style to the racing stroke.

Comparison of the Two Styles

A The Distance Crawl

For distances over 200 yards up to a mile or more, the speed is naturally reduced, and all movements are performed in a more leisurely manner. Because the arm recovery is slower, a slightly increased body roll is required to counter-balance the increased weight of the arm, which, of course, is longer in the air. The body is lower in the water because its slower speed brings the head lower and makes it necessary to submerge the face to the level of the forehead-hair line; and because the head is lower, the body lies flatter on the surface of the water.

B The Sprint Crawl

For distances up to 200 yards, a much faster action is possible and desirable. The swimmer strives to lift his body and glide over the water rather than to plough through it, and because of his greater speed he succeeds at any rate in applying the principle of the hydroplane. Thus he breasts the water and his head is raised so that his eyes are about surface level. He finds it easier to breathe in with only a slight turn of the head, a fact which enables the fast swimmer to adopt the bilateral breathing style which is now recommended by the experts. In this, the swimmer inhales from left and right alternately, as follows:

1 Breathe *in* with head turned to left as you recover your left arm.

2 Breathe *out* with head centred while you recover your right and again your left arm.

3 Breathe *in* with head turned to right as you recover your right arm.

Common Faults in Crawl Swimming

Once you have mastered the basic elements of the crawl, keep on the look-out for ways and means of improving your style. Look especially for these faults:

(i) Too much Splash

This is largely due to faulty entry when the whole arm strikes the water instead of piercing it. In the case of the legs, splash should be avoided by keeping the feet under the water, allowing only the heels to break the surface.

(ii) A Snake-like Action of the Body

This is due to two causes: (*a*) failing to enter and pull in the correct line—that is, pulling out of line—and (*b*) turning the head too vigorously from side to side.

(iii) Burrowing under Water with the Head

This is due to a mistaken conception of the true position.

(iv) Too Narrow or Too Wide Leg Action

Both these are bad faults; too narrow a leg action results in lack of power and too wide an action causes drag.

(v) All Movements too Fast

This is the commonest of all faults, especially among learners, and the cure is an obvious one!

CHAPTER VI

The Back Crawl

In all its main essentials, the Back Crawl closely resembles the Front Crawl. Its timing is practically the same—six leg beats to the complete arm cycle. Its leg action is very similar—the legs working in opposition with an up and down movement. In addition, there is a great similarity between the methods and practices by which the stroke may be learned. Even though it is the fastest back stroke yet discovered, the Back Crawl is a slower stroke than the Front Crawl; this is probably due to the fact that when you are swimming on your back, the arms are at a mechanical disadvantage. They cannot, without causing excessive roll of the body, concentrate their pull in the most effective direction, that is, in a line parallel to the long axis of the swimmer's body.

As a pleasant change from the front crawl there is no other stroke more suitable or more enjoyable to perform because, quite apart from its merits as a racing stroke, it is perhaps one of the easiest and most comfortable strokes in the swimmer's repertoire. Those who can already swim the front crawl will, therefore, find the back crawl comparatively easy to learn. There are naturally a number of minor features which have to be studied if one wishes to become a real expert at the stroke, but with intelligent observation and regular and systematic practice this, like all the other swimming strokes, can soon be mastered.

Position of the Body

The body lies in the water as near to the surface as possible, the head being raised very slightly as if propped up on a low pillow. In order to maintain the horizontal position—the position offering the least resistance to progress when swimming—it is necessary to extend the legs slightly to prevent the knees from bending and to lift the hips a little in an effort to keep the waist-line as near to the surface as possible; this will prevent the legs from sinking and causing drag. Apart from the above, which necessarily involves some muscular action, the body should be quite relaxed and the natural curves of the spine maintained.

The Leg Beat or Thrash

You will recall that in the front crawl the leg action involves a bending at the knee and at the hip-joint and that the emphasis is on the *upward* drive of the lower leg. Now in the back crawl there is a difference, for if you allow a bending in the hip-joint, your knee would be lifted out of the water and its weight would upset your body balance. Remember this point and you will not make the mistake of assuming, as many do, that the leg action of the back crawl is simply an inverted crawl kick. Let us consider what really happens. The foot is lowered in the water to a depth of 18–20 inches, the ankle being stretched so that resistance is felt on the sole of the foot. At the bottom of the movement, the lower leg should form an angle of about 45 degrees with the surface of the water; a greater angle than this would form a drag.

Much of this movement, as you will have observed, occurs at the knee joint, but a really effective leg drive actually involves a movement at the hip joint, that is, a slight lowering of the thigh. The upward movement is like a kick, the pressure being felt on the instep and shin. The toes, by the way, should be turned inwards as in the front crawl and they should just break the surface at the top of the movement.

In order to obtain the fullest power from this action, the

legs must, of course, work in opposition, one leg going down as the other comes up, and both working in such proximity that the knees and toes almost rub together as they pass each other. Keep the legs fairly straight all the time, but the knees and ankles should be relaxed; the toes should be stretched—but not too stiffly.

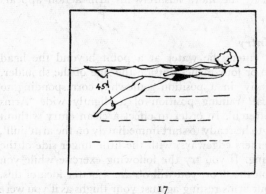

17

The Arm Action of the Back Crawl

Roughly speaking, each arm describes a circular motion, half of which is in the water and half out; or it may provide a better picture if you imagine the arm revolving round the shoulder joint like the spoke of a wheel. Again roughly speaking, the arms are kept in diametric alignment with one another; as one arm enters the water, the other is withdrawn. Because of the physical restriction of certain movements at the shoulder joint it is not possible, without undue body rolling, to dig deep down in the water and to pull with the arm, along the line of the swimmer's progression. In fact, if excessive body roll is to be avoided, it is not usually possible, however supple the swimmer may be, to take the hand lower than about 18 inches at any point of the pull.

D*

Thus the pull must always be along a line which tends to throw the body somewhat out of line and calls for a counter-balancing or compensatory movement of the legs and hips. Like all swimming movements, except perhaps those of the 'Butterfly' breast stroke, the arms in the back crawl move comparatively slowly, and the more expert the swimmer, the more leisurely his arm action appears to be.

(i) The Entry

The hand enters the water at a point beyond the head some three or four inches outside the line of the shoulder, that is to say, in a position somewhat corresponding to the physical training position of a slightly wide 'Arms Upward Stretch'. In order to effect a clean entry without splash and to be ready to start immediately on the arm 'pull', the hand enters edgeways, with the little finger side of the hand leading. If you try the following exercise while you are lying on the floor, you will obtain a better idea of this.

With your arms resting against your thighs as if you were standing to 'attention', raise them forward and upward, turning the palms of the hands outwards while doing so. Continue the movement until the little finger side of the hands touch the floor. You will find that if you have kept your arms straight, your hands, unless you have exceptionally supple shoulders, will be rather wider apart than the shoulder width. This, then, is the point of entry, with a straight arm and the palm turned outwards.

(ii) The Arm Pull

As soon as the arm is under the water the pull commences, and it continues with a strong sweep like the pull of an oar until the hand comes to rest against the side of the thigh. The depth of the pull is extremely important, for if you pull too deeply there is bound to be a loss of power, due to the fact that for much of the time the paddle—the hand—is pressing either downward or upward, and thus dissipating its force. If, however, the arm pull is too shallow, there is a risk of the hand side-slipping out of the water, especially if the water is the least bit choppy. Most of our foremost swimming coaches today recommend a fairly shallow pull to a depth of not more than 12 inches, which would be approximately the deepest one could pull without causing body roll. When the arm has travelled about half its distance, you will see that the 'pull' becomes a 'push,' and it is at this point that the greatest power can—and and should—be applied.

(iii) The Arm Recovery

Although the back crawl has been popular as a racing stroke for a great many years, and consequently has been worked upon by all the finest coaches in the world, there is still a wide difference of opinion amongst them as to the best method of recovering the arm from the water. All are agreed, however, that the arm should be as relaxed as possible and should be carried over reasonably quickly. Let us see where they differ by examining the three methods of recovery which are being taught today by our leading experts.

(a) The Straight Arm High Recovery

This is probably the most popular of the three, although it is thought by many to appear rather mechanical and unnecessarily tiring to the swimmer. In this method, the arm is carried over without any bend in the elbow, although the wrist and fingers are relaxed. The arm is carried high, as in 'Arms forward and upward raise'.

(b) The Bent Arm Recovery

Opponents of this method claim that it reduces the weight-leverage of the arm, and consequently permits of too much body roll. The method, however, is pleasing to the eye, for it looks extremely graceful when it is correctly performed and it certainly gives full scope for relaxation. The elbow is this time carried high sideways, the forearm and hand following in such a manner that the back of the hand passes within a few inches of the side of the face. There is a final flick to straighten the arm for the 'entry'.

(c) The Straight Arm Low Recovery

In this method, the arm is carried round within a few inches of the surface of the water, palm downwards. It is claimed that this method gives the fullest possible correction to the tendency to roll created by the pulling arm, but, like the first method, it makes the stroke appear somewhat mechanical or wooden.

Perhaps the best advice to the beginner is this: if you wish to swim merely for pleasure, learn the bent arm method; if for speed, use the straight low method. If, however, you wish to be really expert at the game, learn all three and then adapt them to the particular occasion.

(iv) The Position of the Head

It can easily be seen that if the head is kept too low in the water, the water will wash over the swimmer's face and make it difficult for him to breathe. On the other hand, if the head is held too high, it will cause the back to be excessively rounded and, possibly, the hips to sink and cause drag. Just as in the front crawl where the fast swimmer raises his head to 'breast' the surface (the hydro-planing principle) so also in the back crawl the swimmer, as he acquires more speed, may adjust his head position as required. It would be wise for the beginner, however, during his early lessons to become accustomed to a head position which does not interfere with body poise. The best way to learn this head position is to lie on the back on the floor with the head resting on a book about two inches in thickness. This tilts the head sufficiently to direct

the eyes along a line which will make an angle of between
45 degrees and 60 degrees with the surface of the water.

(v) Breathing

As the nose and mouth are kept constantly out of the
water, due partly to the tilting of the head and partly to
the fact that the bow-wave made by the head leaves a
convenient trough, it is not necessary to time the rate or
co-ordinate the breathing to the mechanics of the stroke.
All the same, most swimmers find it natural to breathe in
and out with each complete cycle of movements, breathing
in as one arm is carried over (or recovered) and *out* with
the other. If the learner will follow the general rules for
breathing when swimming—breathe deeply, regularly, and
as easily as possible—he will not go far wrong.

Common Faults in the Back Crawl

1 *Too much Splash*

This is a fault common to all beginners. It is wasteful of
energy, besides looking bad and amateurish. Splashing is
due to many causes, the chief of which are: knees and/or
feet lifted out of the water; movements too hurried; faulty
arm entry.

2 *Head too High*

This causes the hips to sink and the knees to bend, with
consequent loss of body poise, leading to loss of speed.

3 *Excessive Body Roll*

This is usually due to the attempt to dig down too deeply
with the arms during the 'pull'.

4 *Over-Reaching*

This fault occurs when the swimmer tries to make his
arm entry as far forward as possible. It causes the shoulder
to be raised and the body to take on a snake-like twist
which, of course, impedes progression.

5. *Failing to keep the Toes Turned in*

This fault is a fairly common one in both the front and back crawls and results in much loss of power, due to the fact that the legs are allowed to move away from one another and therefore to cease working in co-operation. It is the close wedge-like or scissor action which is mainly responsible for imparting the leg drive.

Home Preparation

As you become more and more proficient as a swimmer, you will find that the need for special preparatory exercises on land becomes less and less important. There are, however, one or two movements and positions which can be practised with advantage even by the best of swimmers, if only as a test of their progress and as a check to make sure that they are working along the right lines.

(a) Position of the Head

This has already been described, but it is mentioned again here as a reminder that the head should be raised on a book or cushion whenever home exercises in the lying position are practised.

(b) The Leg Action

It is quite impossible to obtain the true 'feel' of the leg thrash on land, or even, without special suspension apparatus such as a hammock with leg holes, to get the true *movement* of the legs. The only real purpose which can be served by leg drills is that of giving the learner some idea of the six-beat cycle, that is, six beats of the legs to the two arm movements.

(c) The Arm Action—Lying

If you lie on your back on the edge of a bed with your head on a low pillow, you may gain some early assistance from the practice of the arm movements for the Entry, Pull and Catch. Remember that the entry should be made with a straight arm and that the hand should be turned edgeways so that the little finger side of the 'blade' enters first. Try the three methods of recovering the arm and decide which one you will use when you next visit the pool. Remember also to make your pull no deeper than 12 inches at any point.

(d) The Arm Action—Standing

In order to become acquainted with the double or synchronised arm action, try the combined arm movement in the standing position. Raise one arm, with palm turned outwards, in a position corresponding to that of the entry, leaving the other hanging at your side, palm touching the thigh. Now start both arms moving slowly, the uppermost one coming sideways and downwards for the pull, as the other comes up with palm turned outwards for its recovery. If you can fix yourself up on a low narrow support such as a raised plank, you can, of course, obtain a much better idea of this combined action.

(e) Combined Arm and Leg Action

As has already been explained, the fact that it is practically impossible to perform the true leg action for the back crawl on land makes this practice useful only as a means of acquiring a sense of the rhythm or timing of the stroke. Prop yourself up on a line of cushions stretching from head to hips only, leaving the legs unsupported. Work the legs fairly slowly up and down to a six-beat count, and when you feel that you can keep the movement going automatically, add the arm movements, taking three beats to each arm recovery, that is, six beats to the complete stroke. Do not trouble to decide which leg should commence with which arm, for that problem will resolve itself when you get into the water. Throughout the whole of the pull, the little finger should be in contact with the floor. When you are used to the arm and leg co-ordination, add the breathing— 'In, 2, 3—Out, 2, 3,' etc. And now for your water practices.

Water Practices for the Back Crawl

1 Leg Action

Build up your leg work in the following easy stages:

(a) *With Sculling*

First make sure that you can manage the movement of sculling as described in Chapter III. Then take up a straight back-floating position at the rail, with your toes hooked under it. Start your sculling action and when ready give a gentle push-off with your toes and begin your leg movements, easily and slowly at first to make sure that they are being done correctly. Ask yourself these questions, mentally of course!—

1 Are my knees breaking the surface? (They should not do so).

2 Are my toes turned inwards?

3 Am I keeping my legs close enough together to cause my knees and feet almost to rub together as they pass each other?

4 Is my head position correct?

5 Am I 'sitting down' in the water and thereby causing drag?

6 Are my ankles and knees relaxed?

(b) *With hands on hips or stretched beyond the head*

When you have developed the leg action sufficiently to dispense with the assistance of sculling, practise with your hands on your hips and, later, with them stretched out behind your head, palms upwards, thumbs locked or hooked together. Continue this practice until you can travel at a fair speed for one length of the swimming bath.

2 Arm Action

(a) At the Rail

The easiest method of practising the arm action is with the assistance of a helper who stands on the side of the bath and supports you with a rope looped round your waist. It is possible, however, if you do not mind some slight discomfort, to give yourself the necessary support by hooking your toes under the rail and using your feet as levers, by pressing against the side of the bath with your heels. Practise slowly at first, using the following mental catechism:

1. Am I making a clean entry with the little finger side of my hand?
2. Is my entry too wide or too narrow?
3. Am I pulling too deeply?
4. Am I rolling or wriggling my body?
5. Is my head position correct?

(b) With Legs supported by a Float

Unless the legs are supported in some way, it will not be possible to concentrate on the arm action without running the risk of leg-drag. For this reason, and in order to give strong exercise for the arms, the use of a float of some sort will be found helpful. There is danger in using a float for the legs only, however, especially to the in-experienced swimmer, who must be warned not to tie or strap the float to his feet or ankles, but rather to hold it between the feet so that it can be released immediately. The inflated rubber ring or the cork slab are equally useful for this purpose.

Combined Arm and Leg Action

The bringing together of the movements of arms and legs can now be attempted, and, assuming that the previous practices have been well and adequately followed, it should not be a difficult matter to learn the co-ordination. You will find that, at the beginning of your work on this combined practice, it will be easiest for you to start each attempt with a push-off from the rails, then getting your leg movements under way, and finally adding your arm movements. As you swim, think about such things as the position of the head, breathing, and the poise of the body, as you find you are able to pay attention to such things. For the rest, well—just go on practising until you can swim the back crawl for at least half a mile without discomfort or fatigue. Finally, when you can do that, you can afford to give some further attention to speed.

CHAPTER VII

The Dolphin Butterfly Stroke

The Dolphin Butterfly is a tiring and exhausting stroke and it should only be tackled after you have become competent in the other swimming strokes. To be proficient, it requires strength, mobility and good watermanship. Because of these factors, it offers a challenge to anyone who wishes to consider himself an all-round swimmer.

As well as being a competitive stroke in its own right, the Butterfly is used extensively in the training programmes of all swimmers, to build up strength and endurance and to increase mobility. The breast stroke leg kick is sometimes used and is, indeed, permitted by the laws of competitive swimming. This type of kick, however, has a retarding effect on progress forward, so it is rarely seen in competitions. In this chapter, we shall deal exclusively with the Dolphin kick, which over the years has proved to be a much faster and a much more efficient movement.

General Description

In this stroke, all movements of the arms and legs must be simultaneous and symmetrical. The arms must recover over the water together, while the legs must move together, either in the vertical or in the horizontal plane. Because of these factors, the Butterfly is not as fast as the crawl type strokes. In both front and back crawl we have a more or less continuous propulsion forward; one arm is in the water propelling while the other is recovering. In the Butterfly, as in the breast stroke, both arms propel the body forward simultaneously; this is then followed by a loss of propulsion as both arms recover together.

Position of Body

The body should be as nearly horizontal as possible, with the head held naturally, and the eyes looking forward and downward, as in the front crawl. If the shoulders and hips are allowed to sink too far under the water, it will make it very difficult to recover the arms correctly.

Leg Action of the Dolphin Butterfly

The leg action is similar to that already described for the front crawl, but in this case both legs work together instead of in opposition. The legs are raised to the surface of the water, with the knees bending and spreading a little as the feet near the surface. From this position, the legs are driven downwards, and as they near the end of the down beat they are straightened vigorously; this gives a tremendous whip to the feet. The up stroke is started with the legs straight and again the knees bend and spread occurs as the feet near the surface. Throughout the kick, the feet should be relaxed, turned in slightly, and extended backwards.

As the legs kick down, the hips rise, and as the legs return to the surface the hips sink. This is a natural balancing effect, and it gives the stroke its fish-like appearance. The main purpose of the leg kick is to stop the legs from sinking and to keep the body as near horizontal as possible, thus reducing retardation and allowing the powerful action of the arms to pull the body through the water.

Arm Action

(i) Entry

The hands enter the water at a point just inside the shoulders, with the arms extended but not rigidly. The thumbs enter the water first, and as the hand enters, the fingers are turned down and the hand is cupped.

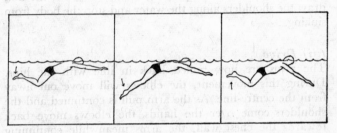

1 Arms entering.
2 Legs starting first kick.

1 Arm starting pull.
2 First leg kick completed.
3 Head still in water and body flat.

1 Arms continue pull.
2 Legs rising to surface.
3 Head still in water.

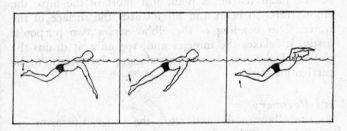

1 Arms under shoulders.
2 Legs starting second kick.

1 Arms starting to recover.
2 Second kick completed.
3 Mouth starting to come clear of surface for breathing.
4 Body flat.

1 Arm recovery above surface, shoulders high as possible.
2 Legs rising to surface.

18—Sequence and timing of the Dolphin Butterfly Stroke

(ii) Catch

This occurs almost immediately. As soon as the hands are in the water, start pressing down; this will lift and draw the shoulders along the water and stop the body from sinking.

(iii) Drive

The arms are now pulled back in line with the hips. During this movement, the elbows will move out away from the centre-line. As the arm pull is continued and the shoulders come over the hands, the elbows move back towards the chest wall, the arms meanwhile continuing their drive back towards either hip. There are no pauses in the movement. The hand and arm are continuously contributing to the task of propelling the body forward.

(iv) Release

As the hand reaches a point just short of the hips, the elbow starts to bend and lift towards the surface of the water. This bending of the elbow serves two purposes; firstly, it relaxes the muscles and, secondly, it drains the water off the arms, thereby reducing the weight to be carried forward.

(v) Recovery

As the elbow and hand clear the water, the arms are rotated and swing forward in a low lateral sweeping movement. The body and shoulders should be kept high in the water whilst the arms are recovering.

Breathing

Inhalation should normally take place during the later part of the arm drive, or even during the first part of the arm recovery. The exact point will depend upon the strength and power of the arm drive. The head should be kept as low as possible and not unduly lifted backwards. If the head is lifted too much, it will cause the legs to sink, making recovery much more difficult. To minimise this loss of poise, breathing can take place every second stroke, or else the head can be turned to the side for inhalation by rotating the head, similar to the front crawl. The explosive breathing technique should be used, the breath being forcibly exhaled through nose and mouth as the mouth is coming clear of the water.

Timing

The ideal timing is two leg beats to one continuous arm pull. The first beat is made as the hands reach catch-point and first start their pull. The second beat is made as the elbows start to move backwards towards the chest wall and the arms begin their drive back towards the hips.

Home Preparation for the Butterfly

Like the front crawl, the Butterfly is best suited for water practice. The exercises listed below, however, will help to increase the mobility of the shoulders, which is such an important factor in Butterfly swimming. A little time spent daily on these exercises will greatly assist your water practices.

1 Stand upright with your feet apart. Now circle your arms forward, keeping them straight throughout. Try to make the shoulder blades meet at the back, and brush your ears with your upper arms on the way forward.

2 Repeat the exercise above, but this time circle the arms backward.

3 In this exercise you need a piece of rope about five feet long. Stand upright and hold the rope above your head, with your arms spread as far apart as possible. Keeping your arms straight and the rope taut, force your arms

as far backward as you can. Do this about ten times, then move the hands a few inches closer and repeat the exercise.

Water Practice for the Butterfly

A Leg Action

Work up your leg action in the following easy stages:

1 *At the Rail*

(a) Hold the side of the bath with both legs extended backwards. Spread the knees a little and bend them to lift the soles of the feet up to the surface of the water. Now, moving the legs from the hips, vigorously flick the legs down to a depth of about eighteen inches. Remember to keep the feet extended, relaxed and pointing slightly inwards. Lift the legs back to the surface, allowing the knees to spread and bend as the feet approach the surface.

(b) Repeat the above practice, but with a faster action, without letting the legs bend unduly. Keep the feet under water the whole time, trying to obtain a whip-like action. You will find that, as you kick down, your hips will rise, and as you lift the legs up, the hips will sink. This is a natural action and reaction balancing effect.

2 *Arms stretched above the head*

(a) Take a deep breath and push off in the glide position with arms stretched forward. Do as many dolphin kicks as you can; when you want to breathe, use a breast stroke arm action to lift your head up to enable you to breathe in. Lower your face back in the water and, keeping your arms forward, carry on with another series of kicks. Continue this method across the width of the pool.

(b) Hold a float stretched out in front of you. Keep your

face in the water, only lifting it to breathe, and practise
your kick.

B Arm Action

1 Stand in shallow water, with one foot a good walking
pace in front of the other. Now lean forward and lower
your shoulders under water, with your arms stretched
forward. You can now practise the arm action. Keep
asking yourself the following questions:

(a) Are my hands entering thumbs first?

(b) Are my hands entering the water at a point just inside
the shoulders, or are they too wide?

(c) Are my hands smashing into the water or are they
merely dropping in?

(d) Am I driving my arms backwards continuously in a
pulling and pushing action?

(e) Am I bending my elbows at the release point?

(f) Am I recovering my arm forward as fast as possible
as soon as my hands are clear of the water?

2 For this practice you need the assistance of a helper,
who stands on the bath side and supports you with a rope
looped under your chest. You can now practise your arm
action, still asking yourself the same questions as in the
previous practice.

C Combining Arm and Leg Action

At this stage we first introduce a glide after each arm action.
This will prove less tiring than the continuous action of the
arms and will also give you more time to think of what you
are doing.

First push off from the wall in the glide position, make
two leg beats, then one pull, and recover the arms forward.
Repeat the two leg beats and again pull and recover the
arms. You will have noticed by this time that when the
legs are moving the arms are extended forward and kept

still, and that when the arms are moving, the legs are extended backwards and kept still. Do not be tempted to go too far at first; stand up after the second arm pull.

It now requires constant practice, gradually increasing the distance swum. When you are able to swim two hundred yards by this method, you can afford to think of further speed. To go faster, we have obviously to cut out the glide after each arm pull; you will find this extremely tiring at your first attempt.

Start by cutting down the distance to be swum. Be content to swim across the width of the swimming pool, or even half a width if it is a wide pool. Concentrate upon a continuous action of the arms; as soon as the hands enter the water, press down to catch-point and start the arm drive. Do not worry about the legs at first, but concentrate upon the heaving action of the arms. Hold your breath at first, only breathing when necessary. As your strength and endurance improve, increase the distance covered, fitting in the leg beats as described in the earlier paragraph on Timing.

CHAPTER VIII

Learning to Dive

Introduction

Diving is another of the water arts which is administered
by the Amateur Swimming Association. Originally, there
was a separate Amateur Diving Association, but this was
merged into the A.S.A. shortly before the Second World
War. Championships are staged each year by the various
County, District, and, of course, National Associations.
Those who wish to teach themselves to dive should try to
attend one of these championship meetings and watch
very carefully the execution of the various dives. So, first
of all, let us go along to one of these events and see what
happens.

The Championship will obviously have certain conditions laid down—which boards will be used, what dives
will be performed, and so on—but our guide will be the
referee. He will announce the types of dives at the beginning
and will then point out to us where the judges are sitting.
Each judge—and there can be from three to five of them—
has taken up a different position on the edge of the bath.
He has in his hand a set of cards numbered from 1 to 10,
with half numbers from 5 upwards. The referee announces
the first diver; he blows a whistle and the diver steps on to
the board and performs the dive. Incidentally, the dive
starts from the moment the diver takes up his position, and
it finishes when he has completely disappeared under the
surface. When the referee is sure that all the judges have
had time to make their decisions, he blows his whistle
again and each judge simultaneously holds up a card

showing his award. These numbers are noted down by
the Recorder, who keeps a running total so that he can
say within a very short time at the end of the competition
who is the winner. If it is a Fancy Diving Competition,
the procedure is varied from the Recorder's point of view,
since each dive has its 'difficulty factor.' This is set down
in a Tariff, and the awards of the judges must be multiplied
by this tariff value to obtain the final figure.

All this, and many other minor but interesting points,
will be noted by our would-be diver, and once the
Championships are over, it is *his* turn; so off we go down
to the local Baths. The Diving Boards, incidentally, should
be built to an international standard. Their heights and
lengths, and the depth of the water below them, too, are
all regulated by the F.I.N.A. (Federation Internationale
de Natation Amateur) and all measurements are therefore
in metres. The principal boards are at 1 metre (approximately 3 ft. 3 in.), 3 metres (9 ft. 10 in.), 5 metres (16 ft. 4 in.)
and 10 metres (32 ft. 7 in.). So, casting a longing glance at
the structure arising at the deep end, we wend our way
along the bath to the shallower water, for that is where
we are going to begin. You are no stranger to the water,
because we are assuming that you have performed at least
some of the exercises mentioned in the first part of this book,
and that you can manage, even if it is in a rather peculiar
method, to progress along the surface of the water. Up to
this point you have been concentrating on keeping yourself
on the surface; now you will rapidly find that it is difficult
not to remain on the surface!

Surface Dives—Land and Water Drill

First of all, try out this sequence on dry land:

(*a*) Stand with your feet together and your arms stretched
out in front of you, in the old 'Arms Forward Stretch'
position of your P.T. days.

(b) Bend the trunk forward very slightly and bend the knees somewhat, as if you were going to spring up.

(c) Breathe in and bend your head as far forward as possible.

(d) Bring your arms sideways and back, and bend at the hips as much as possible. This places you in the 'pike' or 'jack-knife' position.

(e) Use your arms as in the dog-paddle and gradually assume position (a).

This is the same movement exactly which you will carry out in the water, except that the dive will be continued to its logical conclusion and your feet will leave the bottom of the bath. So let us try it in water about three or four feet deep.

(a) Take up the position as described before—feet together and arms 'forward stretch'.

(b) Bend the trunk forward and bend the knees, so that this time your shoulders are just under the surface of the water.

(c) Breathe in and bend your head forward, putting your face in the water.

(d) Bring your arms sideways and back and, letting your body adopt an inverted V position, push off with your feet from the bottom of the bath.

(e) Scull with your hands and arms. This will propel you down through the water and up again to a standing position.

All these individual movements should be practised until you can do a reasonable surface dive and until you get the idea of going under the water in a head-first position.

Surface Dives—Advanced

The surface dive is one which is used in Life-Saving, when an object—possibly a body—is to be brought up from the

19—Surface Dive

bottom of the bath. We are not concerned in this chapter with the salvaging of objects from the bottom, so we will only describe the dive and the return to the surface without any added weight to be carried. It is, of course, performed in these circumstances as a continuous movement when one is swimming. In this way, you can obtain a very powerful push under the surface by timing the dive to take place as the legs are performing the 'kick' of the breast stroke. When you sweep your legs out and round, your head should be submerged and your arms extended together towards the bottom. As the legs complete their circuit and come together, the arms should make a strong breast-stroke movement. The body is then tilted towards the bottom, and an added impetus is given to its rapid submersion by lifting the legs vertically into the air in line with the descending body.

To return to the surface, all that is necessary is to change the direction of the thrust by raising the head and arms; then give a vigorous sweep-back with the arms and out will pop your head. As you are still in shallow water, your feet will naturally come to rest on the bottom of the bath. If you should be in deep water, as soon as your head emerges, continue your original swimming stroke along the surface.

Sitting Dives

This is a section which the adult learner may think rather beneath him; but it is an admirable way of introducing oneself to a head-first entry from a small height above the water. To call it a dive is really rather magnifying its importance, because all you will do here is to learn how to fall in neatly and without fuss. Choose a part of the bath in which you already feel at home when swimming, nearer the shallow end, and then:

(a) Sit on the side with your heels together on the bar. You must sit as near the edge as possible.

(b) Keep your heels together and open your knees as wide as possible.

(c) Lean your head forward and raise your arms to that they meet above your head.

(d) Now, keeping your head cradled in your arms, tilt your body forward until you fall in. At the moment of falling, your knees should still be wide open and your heels should still be on the bar.

(e) As you enter the water, bring your knees together and see if you can make a clean entry. Because your hands and arms are outstretched, they will be the first point of contact with the bottom, so be prepared either (i) to let your feet drop to the bottom of the bath and so stand up, or (ii) to start a swimming stroke and so continue along the surface of the water. By changing the angle at which your arms are held, you will also change the direction of your movement through the water.

Practise these falls into the water until you are quite

adept at the job of recovering your balance at the earliest possible moment after submersion. The next stage is the first standing dive.

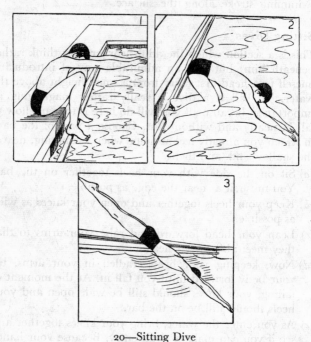

20—Sitting Dive

Elementary Standing Dives

There is a distinct possibility that you are going deeper now, so it would be advisable to leave the shallow end and proceed up the bath a little way. Take up a position on the side, with your toes actually lapping over the edge, legs together, body upright, hands by your side, eyes looking straight ahead. In that position, you are ready to carry out the following sequence:

(a) Arms forward stretch; bend your head so that it is again cradled in your arms.

(b) Lean forward over the water and raise one leg behind you in line with your body.

(c) Go on leaning forward until you topple over into the water. As you go, give a little spring with the foot that is just leaving the side.

(d) This 'one-legged' dive will send you head first into the water, and the act of bringing the leg up behind will give your dive the necessary steepness.

21—Elementary Standing Dive

The most important part of this practice dive is to make a clean entry into the water. Try and mark a spot on the surface at which to aim yourself. Then imagine that that spot is a round hole through which all your body must pass. In other words, your feet will eventually go through the hole made by your hands on the surface of the water.

As you improve on this first dive, other points will bring themselves to your notice. It is important that the body should be in a straight line from the fingertips to the toes. Hands must be outstretched, the head tucked securely between the arms, with the eyes still looking straight ahead, the toes must be pointed, and the feet 'jammed' together. All these things will come with practice. Now let us pass on to the next stage—our first real dive.

E

The Plain Header

First of all, it is a good thing to enlarge on the one-legged dive, in which you are by this time more proficient, by toppling in without raising the leg behind you. That is to say, stand as before with your toes overlapping the edge, lean forward, and topple over into the water, trying to keep both legs together. We are now ready to start our first recognised dive, the 'plain header'.

Stand upright on the edge of the bath, with your feet together and toes overlapping the edge. Raise the arms sideways, mid-way between the head and the shoulders, with the palms of the hands facing forwards. The head is held erect, with the eyes looking straight forward. This is the starting position; when seen from the front, it resembles the letter Y.

From the starting position, the weight is transferred to the balls of the feet by allowing the knees to bend slightly. As the knees bend, the trunk leans slightly forward, but take care that the hips remain over the feet. Now straighten the legs vigorously and drive the hips upward. Because after the slight leaning forward of the trunk as you go upwards, the body will tilt over into the entry position. In your flight through the air, your legs must be straight and your toes pointed. The arms remain mid-way until just prior to the entry, when they are brought together above the head.

The entry should be as near vertical as possible, with the whole body passing through the hole that your hands have made in the water.

For your first few attempts, take up the starting position as described above and lean the trunk right forward as in Diagram 22, remembering to keep your hips over your feet. From this position, quickly bend and stretch the knees to drive the hips up. Try to bring the entry a little closer to the bath-side with each subsequent attempt.

As you become more proficient, gradually decrease the

amount of lean forward, until you are able to perform the dive from an almost upright position. The important thing is to drive the hips up and make sure that the legs follow the same path.

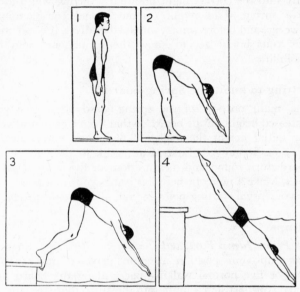

22—The Plain Header

A good tip is to imagine that there is a small fence over which you have to dive. As the hips pass over the fence, lift the legs backward, so that the body is straight from the tips of the fingers to the toes, and stretch out for the entry. When you feel that you can perform this dive satisfactorily, go up the bath and try it in the deep water. You will find it much easier there as you have more scope and you will eventually develop more confidence in making a vertical entry.

Then, if you are fortunate enough to have a properly

equipped bath, go on to the low springboard. This should be the 'one metre board.' Take up your stance at the end of the board and repeat the dive. You will find that the board will give you a lot of assistance in bringing your body into the correct flight position by giving you a little extra spring. This requires some special consideration, however, and before you try any further dives, it is essential that you should get to know the springboard and its possibilities.

Getting to know the Spring-board

The main purpose of the spring-board is to give you increased height off the board, so that from a comparatively low initial height the angles of flight and entry can be more easily gauged. First of all, walk to the end of the board, turn round and measure four or five normal paces back. Make a note of where this brings you; that point will be your usual starting point in your springboard dives.

Jumps

(i) Plain Jump Forward

Take up your position at your 'personal' mark. Take four or five normal walking paces along the board and make your last step a jump into the air so that you land on the end of the board with both feet together. As you do this, slightly bend your knees and ankles and drop your arms to your sides. The board will give slightly, and, as it rises, you should spring up and out; keep your body as straight as possible—your arms will help you in this—and you will enter the water feet first.

The most difficult part of this movement to master is the final jump or 'hurdle' step. This is the key to the whole art of springboard diving, and it must be conscientiously practised; so here it is in detail:

(a) As the jump is taken, swing your arms forwards and up.

(b) Continue the swing until the arms are above the level of the head and at the sides, at an angle of 45 degrees above the horizontal at the highest point of the jump.

(c) The end of the board should be watched, and when the feet touch, the head should be raised so that the body is erect.

(d) As the feet touch the board, the arms should be swung outwards, slightly back, and downwards. The full weight of the body will now depress the board and we are ready to commence the rise.

(e) The swing of the arms forwards and upwards now begins, and the knees and ankles, which have been slightly bent, now straighten to assist the spring.

(f) The feet leave the board as the arms carry their swing up past the face. The body is upright and in a straight line from toes to fingertips.

(g) As the descent—feet-first—commences, bring the arms tight in to the sides.

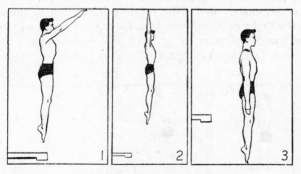

23—Plain Jump Forward

Remember to adjust your movements to the movements of the board; the board will help you only if you do not fight against it! Your hurdle step must be taken as the board directs, and it must be timed so that both you and the board are moving in the same direction. Try to obtain a rhythm in your complete movements all through your dive. There are many variations of this first training jump which we have tried as above, but we will concentrate on three further jumps only before attempting the first running dive.

24—The Hurdle Step

(ii) Haunch Jump Forward

Proceed exactly as for the previous jump, but at the top of the flight draw up your legs, lower your arms, and grip the middle of your shins. Keep this position for a split second, holding as compact a 'tuck' as possible. Straighten

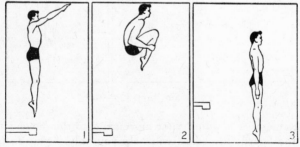

25—Haunch Jump Forward

the body out and enter the water feet first as before. There are two points to watch in this jump—(*a*) make sure you grip the middle of the shins, and (*b*) do not get into this haunch position until you have reached the highest point of your jump.

(iii) Pike Jump Forward

In simple language, your job this time is to touch your toes at the highest point of your jump. Just before the top of the flight, bring your legs up to the horizontal, bring the arms down, and reach forward to touch the tips of the toes. Hold it for a split second, then lower the legs, straighten the body, and enter the water feet first. The point to watch is the same as before: do not adopt this position until you have reached your 'ceiling.'

26—Pike Jump Forward

(iv) Backward Jump

Take up your position on the end of the board with your back to the water. Your spring is going to be from the balls of the feet, so your weight should be resting on them, with your heels projecting over the end of the board. As your arms are moved rapidly up past your face, jump upwards and backwards. Whip your arms down to your sides, point the toes, and enter the water feet first. Do not lean too far back with your take-off.

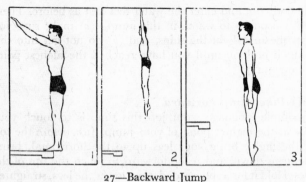

27—Backward Jump

Dives from the Spring-board

When you have thoroughly mastered the 'feel' of the board, when you can synchronise your movements with those of the board, and when you can obtain real height from your hurdle step, then it is time to try 'bouncing' the board. In this practice you do everything mentioned in the detail of the hurdle step—you take your walk of four or five paces along the board and you make your hurdle step. But this time you jump on the end of the board and allow it to send you vertically up in the air, or a little back from the vertical. This means that you will land again on the board with both feet as the board also is descending. Then, as the board rises, you will launch yourself up into the air again. These movements must be timed to fit in with those of the board, and the bounce can be repeated two or three times. For each successive rise, your arms should go through the same motions as described in the hurdle step detail. Practice at this bouncing will lead you to gain greater confidence in the board, together with a greater height off it. Height from the board is now our great aim as we come to try the first and most popular of all 'show dives'—the Swallow. It goes

28—Swallow

under various names, but in strict Diving parlance it is
known as a *Header Forward, Straight*.

E*

Proceed along the board with your usual number of paces and make your hurdle step a decisive one, so that your take-off will be upwards and slightly outwards. The arms swing forwards and upwards as in the English Header, but instead of going beyond the head, the swing is outwards and backwards until they are level with, and in line with, the shoulders. This position should be reached just after the highest point of your flight and should be held until just before you enter the water. Whilst in the position, keep the head up and hold the legs well back; the feet should be slightly above the level of the head at the beginning of the position. As you prepare to enter the water, drop the head forward and close the arms alongside it—that is, in the final position of the ordinary header—and once again enter in a vertical position.

It is essential that you obtain plenty of height from the board and that, of course, the dive should be regarded as a complete entity. The movements must be smooth and continuous—almost leisurely, in fact!

Fancy Spring-board Diving

Spring-board dives are many in number and to describe all of them fully would not really come within the scope of this book. So we will select certain 'key' dives and some of the simpler 'fancy' dives. So far, we have managed without any help from coaches or friends on the side; but now I do seriously advise the would-be championship diver to consider joining a club which has a good diving coach. For those who do not aspire to championship form, it would be a great help if you can persuade a friend to stand on the side and give helpful criticism. There is an old saying that the spectator sees more of the game, and it is very true, of course, in diving.

For easy classification, the springboard dives are divided into 5 groups:

1 *Forward dives from a forward take-off* are dives begun with the body facing the water. The plain header comes into this class.

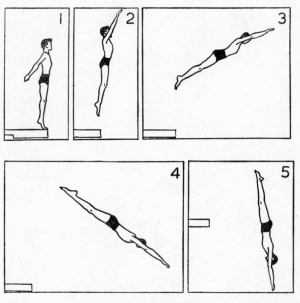

29—Header Forward

2 *Backward dives from a backward take-off* are commenced with the body facing the board and with the back to the bath. The take-off is very near to the vertical.

3 *Backward dives from a forward take-off*, that is, 'reverse' dives, are commenced with the body facing the water. The take-off is as for a plain dive, but the feet rise to the front and you enter the water with your back to the main bath and face to the bank.

30—Header Backward

4 *Inward Dives*—Forward dives from a backward take-off are usually referred to as 'inward dives.' The dive is commenced with the body facing the board. The take-off is again almost vertical, but the water is entered with the body facing down the bath.

5 *Screw or Twist dives* are those in which the body turns

laterally in addition to its forward or backward movements, that is to say, it turns also on an axis which is a line drawn through your body from head to toes. The body can do a complete revolution or merely a half-twist. For example, a plain forward header with a half-twist will make you enter the water as from a back dive; with a full twist, a normal entry would be made.

31—Backward Dive, forward take-off

32—Inward Dive (Piked)

33—Half Twist Forward

The previous five groups contain altogether sixty dives and, to increase the variety still more, many of them can be performed in two or three 'positions'. These 'positions' are the attitudes taken up in the flight and are quite simple to understand. For convenience, they are always lettered in the same way:

(a) Straight

As already described in the plain header, in which the body is not bent at knees or hips; arms straight and toes pointed. (See Diagrams 23 and 29.)

(b) Pike

As described in the 'pike jump,' in which the body bends at the hips; the legs are kept straight at the knees and the toes pointed. (See Diagram 26.)

(c) With Tuck

As described in the 'haunch jump,' in which the whole body is bunched up, with the knees together, in a compact ball. (See Diagram 25.)

The final entry into the water in all these cases is made with the arms being brought together and stretched above the head to make the body a straight line from top to toe.

Now let us try out some of the more straightforward dives. From the first group, we will take a pike dive, a somersault, and a 1½ somersault, and all three can be done either standing or running.

1 Header Forward with Pike

This is a very simple but effective version of the header forward, which we have already mastered. The take-off is exactly the same as for the plain header. As you are reaching the top of your flight, lift up your hips and bend your body forward, so that you can touch your pointed toes with your fingers. Then, when you reach your greatest height from the board, you will show—and hold for a second—this pike or jack-knife position with your legs still vertical. Your head should be kept up, not lowered; then, as you approach the water, straighten the body out, stretch your arms above your head and tuck your head between them,

34—Header Forward with Pike

entering the water vertically. Do not aim too far away from the board and keep your movements flowing easily and without any sudden jerks.

2 Somersault Forward with Tuck

The easiest position in which to perform this dive is the tuck position. Once again the take-off is as for the plain header. Height is essential, and as you come to the top of your dive, you adopt the most compact tuck position possible. Grip your shins and drop your head forward; this will start your turning. When you are nearly round, straighten out, raise your head, push your legs forward, and you will drop into the water feet first. At the same time

35—Somersault Forward

your arms should be thrust down against your sides. You will find that the main difficulty in these dives is to know when to straighten out, and here you really do need some help at first. Arrange if you can for a friend to watch you and to shout at the exact moment when you should straighten up.

3 1½ Somersault Forward with Tuck

Follow all the instructions as for the previous dive, except that the tuck position is assumed in a far more vigorous manner and the position is held longer until the water is visible. Then the body should be straightened out and you enter the water as in the plain header.

36—Somersault Forward

4 Header Backward—Straight

We will now take one dive from the second group; this of course, is a standing dive. Take up your position on the end of the board as for a backward jump. Your take-off will be much the same except that you must swing your arms forwards and upwards; at the same time, your feet should rise forwards. At the height of your dive, hollow your back and push your head and arms vigorously backwards. This will turn your body over, so that you will enter the water vertically. (See Diagram 30.)

5 Reverse Dive—Straight

We will also take one dive from the third group, and this can be done either standing or running. The take-off is the same as for our plain jump forward until the feet have left the board. Then the back should be hollowed and the chest lifted, while the legs rise forwards and upwards. As you reach the top of your flight force your head and shoulders backward and place your arms in the swallow position. This will turn your body gently down towards the water, which you should enter as in the plain header—vertically, with arms outstretched above your head. (See Diagram 31.)

6 Back-Front Dive—Pike

This is our dive from the fourth group. Start by taking up the stance as for the backward jump. It is essential in this dive to make your take-off well up and backwards. The pike position is reached at the highest point of the flight by keeping the legs vertical and bending the body forward. Touch the toes with the tips of your fingers. Hold the position and then straighten out by lifting the legs up behind and moving the arms to their entry position as in the plain header. Once again the entry is vertical.

7 Half-Twist Dive—Straight

This is merely one of the tremendous possibilities which Group V offers; half-twists and twists can be combined with practically all the dives in the other groups. The dive you are going to perform now follows the same lines as the plain header until you reach the top of your flight. At that point, you lower the left arm, press back the right arm and shoulder, and turn your head to the left. Your body will begin to turn and you should then control the spin until the half-turn is done. Move the head between the arms, which now take up their entry position, and you enter the water vertically with your back to the board as in our Dive No. 4. To achieve a *full* twist, the movement in the air at the top of the flight must be more vigorous and must be helped by swinging the left arm across the chest and making a definite turn with the shoulders. These twist dives can, of course, be performed either way round, according to which way the diver prefers.

Out of the many possible dives, only the previous seven have been described in detail. It should, however, be realised that merely knowing how to do them is not enough. Diving of this nature requires real determination and confidence. You must be decisive in all your movements on the board; to be half-hearted is to invite a resounding 'flat' dive. So the best advice is—always make up your mind exactly what you have to do and—do it!

Some More Dives Worth Trying

Finally, let us consider two serious and several humorous dives. They all look harder than they actually are, and they are therefore very effective, either in small displays or merely to amuse your friends.

A *The Plunge*

The object of this type of dive is to see how far you can

travel in the water, using only the driving power of your
initial take-off. It follows, therefore, that the angle of
entry should be very narrow. Stand on the side and take
a good deep breath. Bend your knees and take up position
with your body bent forward and your arms stretched
back behind you. Swing your arms very vigorously forward
and 'launch' yourself from the side. The thrust should
come from the vigorous push-off given by the toes. You
should aim to enter the water at a distance from the side
which is about twice your own height, and you should
not go deeper than two or three feet below the surface.
A good idea is to plunge 'across' the bath at first, aiming
to reach the other side. Your progress can be gauged by
the parallel lines on the bottom of the bath which mark
the swimming lanes. The correct control of your breathing
is another aid to distance in the plunge. Allow your breath
to escape only very slowly. Another aid is 'abdominal'
breathing—the contraction and expansion of your stomach
muscles will provide a little more gliding distance.
Additional points connected with the plunge are given in
Chapter IX.

37—Plunge

B The Racing Dive
Many a championship depends on the efficient performance
of this dive. In a race, the starter will line up the swimmers
behind their appointed places. He will then say—'Take

your marks.' Thereupon, you step on to the edge of the bath and take up position as for a plunge—toes curled over the edge, knees bent, body leaning forward from the hips, arms held slightly back, and head looking straight forward. The starter will wait until everybody is completely still and then say 'Go.' You then fling your arms forward

38—Racing Dive

until they are above your head in a line with the body, and straighten your legs vigorously so that you shoot out like an arrow over the water. Your angle of entry must be a narrow one, the body not going much more than a foot under the surface. As soon as possible, start your swimming stroke and off you go!

C Comic Dives

(i) Learner's Dive

The higher your take-off position, the more effective is this dive. Take up your stance as for a plain header forward, but with rather exaggerated movements. Then suddenly double up and enter the water head first *very* near to the side, almost creeping over the edge of the bath! This dive can also be done running from a springboard, when the hands should be held together in front of the chest and pointing out towards the water.

(ii) Mis-step

This is a running dive from any board. Carry on exactly the same as for a plain header until you land on the board for the take-off. Instead of landing with two feet, allow one foot to go on the board and the other one under the board as you tilt over. You then enter the water under the board head first in the usual way.

(iii) Jelly-Fish

Proceed once again as for a plain dive—running along the board, making the hurdle step, and getting plenty of height. As soon as your flight commences, wave your arms and legs and 'buck' your body, coming into the normal entry position at the very last moment.

(iv) Bicycle Dive

This must be done from a high fixed board. Run along the board holding your arms as if they were holding the handlebars of an old-fashioned bicycle. Keep them in that position throughout the dive. Jump high in the air from the board and commence to pedal as if you were riding a bicycle. The entry is feet first.

(v) Half a Pike

This is exactly what it says! It is a pike dive in which, instead of both hands touching both feet, only half the position is attained, that is, you grasp one ankle with both hands and allow the other leg to trail behind. You can enter the water still in this position or you can straighten out at the last moment.

There are many other comic dives which can be devised. If they are to be part of an official gala, they are improved, of course, by a running commentary from the side of the bath.

In conclusion, while it is hoped that the jumps and dives described in this chapter will be useful in helping the beginner, it is only fair to say that diving requires a greater degree of confidence than any of the other water arts. Only real hard work and practice can produce a championship standard, but if you carry out the suggestions already outlined, you will reach a standard of diving which is satisfactory to yourself at least, and you will lay the foundations so soundly that with the help of a coach you can aspire to greater things later.

CHAPTER IX

Miscellaneous Water Skills

A Floating

It is generally accepted in swimming circles that 'floating' means lying face upwards at the surface of the water, in a motionless horizontal position. Some people, especially women and children, are able to do this easily in fresh water, and everyone can do so in salt water. It is a matter of density, buoyancy, balance and poise. Some people experience difficulty due to the legs sinking or water flooding over the face and thus interfering with breathing. The following factors have to be considered, as they appear to affect the individual, and there is no doubt that study, with practice, given to them will lead up to the motionless horizontal floating position, and at the same time bring about a general improvement in all aspects of swimming.

A Unalterable Factors
(i) The Density of the Water

Density means the weight of unit volume of a substance, and for pure water this is one gramme per cubic centimetre. Salt water is denser, according to the amount of salt dissolved in the water. The Dead Sea, for example, is so salt that it will support an egg, and the human body will float in it without any effort whatever. So the denser the floating medium, the easier it is to float.

(ii) The Density of the Person

This varies from 0·985 for an average man to 0·950 for women and children. Human density is largely governed by heavy bone and muscle and by the amount of fatty tissue present. A few men whose density is over 1·000 will have the greatest difficulty in floating in fresh water, but in salt water, of density 1·200 or more, the upthrust on the body is greater and hence floating is easier. If we assume an average human density of 0·980, then this as a fraction is 98/100 or 49/50, which means that only one fiftieth of the body can be supported above the water. This is generally the top or back of the head, and if it is desired to lift more than one-fiftieth of the body out of the water, some compensatory action has to take place to counter-balance the increased weight of that part of the body which is above water level. This brings us to consider the question of alterable factors.

B Alterable Factors—Buoyancy

We have to consider next the effects of buoyancy, which is the upthrust of the water upon the body. When a body is placed in water, it is supported by the force of buoyancy acting upwards through the centre of buoyancy. The latter is the centre of the water space which is occupied by the body; it is not the same point as the centre of gravity of the whole body, and therefore we have two forces acting upon the body causing it to move, as in diagram 39a.

Ideally, the centres of gravity and buoyancy should be on the same vertical line, in which case you would float at rest. If the arms are at your side, the centre of gravity is nearer to your feet, which thus tend to sink. But by lifting the arms above the head, the centre of gravity is moved headwards, counteracting this tendency. This can also be assisted by controlling our breathing. If air is inhaled by using the chest muscles to move the ribs and also by depressing the diaphragm at the base of the chest, then the centre of buoyancy will move down towards the stomach, that is, nearer to the centre of gravity, as in diagram 39b above. To breathe correctly means to inhale quickly and deeply, filling the chest cavity right down to the diaphragm, and then to exhale slowly, being ready to inhale again as

soon as buoyancy is felt to be less—that is to say, as soon
as the body starts to sink.

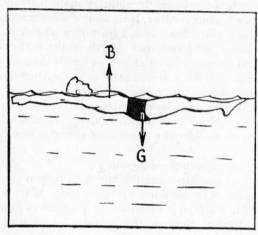

39a

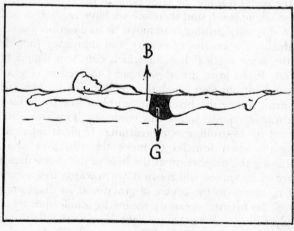

39b

Once these adjustments are understood, the next step is to start with easy practices which will build up to the horizontal position. All the movements should be made slowly, breathing should be carried out correctly, and the body should be kept relaxed, without any undue tenseness; in that way, poise and balance will be preserved. Here are some practices for floating, in an approximate order of difficulty:

(a) *Push off and glide*—face downwards.

(b) *Push off and glide*—face upwards.

(c) *Mushroom Float*

Take a deep breath, pull your knees up to your chest with your hands, and bend the head forward. You will then float with your back and shoulders above the surface, giving the appearance of a mushroom to an onlooker. Now slowly exhale, by bubbling air out into the water, and then stand up when you require to inhale again.

(d) *Letter X face downwards*

Glide forward gently and spread your arms and legs apart to form an X. Exhale slowly again.

(e) *Perpendicular Float*

Tread water gently, breathe steadily, and lift your arms to a sideways position; then lower your head backwards. This is not a true perpendicular position, but it allows normal breathing to take place and also enables the head to be moved in order to adjust balance.

(f) *Letter X face upwards*

Glide gently on the back and spread out the arms and legs to form an X. Breathe steadily and adjust the head position to achieve a balance.

(g) *Horizontal Float*

Take this in three stages, as follows:

1   Assume the back glide position, relaxed, with the feet tucked under the rail, or supported by a small cork float between the ankles. Breathe steadily.

2 Move the arms gently, under the water, to a position beyond the head, so that the thumbs are touching.

3 Release the feet from the rail or float and commence making the necessary adjustments of the fingers and head, lifting them slightly above water level, so that you feel the feet rising. Slacken the knee joints a little. If you have a partner near at hand, you can be given some support under the buttocks. Your partner can also tell you, better than you can see, what effect your adjustments of hands and head position, together with correct breathing, have upon the actual horizontal position you are trying to attain.

(h) *Vertical Float*

The above floating positions have been given in order of difficulty, but the vertical float is one which will require much patience and practice to attain. Once it is mastered, however, it will give you complete confidence in yourself as a swimmer. First tread water out of your depth and scull gently by moving your cupped hands to and fro against the sides of your body. Then inhale deeply and cease all movements of hands and legs. The water level should be just below your mouth and as you exhale slowly it will rise to the lips. At this point, you require to inhale again quickly and deeply, using the full content of your chest cavity right down to the diaphragm. The true vertical position of the body must not be spoilt by a tendency to press the head back.

Generally, to master all the above floating positions requires much perseverance and self-confidence. It is easy to give up, largely due to immersion of the mouth, which causes a learner to struggle instinctively to regain breath. Try to put down any attempt to struggle or fight the water, and you will soon make steady progress.

Now that you understand the principles of floating you should couple this knowledge to sculling and thus be able to carry out many more water skills which will give you pleasure when you have acquired them, as well as a feeling of complete mastery over the water. Let us now consider some of these skills, with brief notes about each in explanation.

B Other Water Skills

1 Sculling Head-First in the Floating Position

The cupped hands are moved to and fro by the sides of the body, pushing the water towards the feet. Sometimes a circular, or figure eight movement is made about the wrists. The upper arms must be kept close to the body, and the minimum movement possible should take place in the forearm, with the maximum movement possible taking place in the wrists.

2 Sculling Feet-First

This is the same as the previous skill, except that the hand movement is reversed, so as to drive water towards the head.

3 Canoe

The body travels head foremost on the chest, using sculling as the propulsive action. Hollow the back, raise the head, and bring the toes to the surface, thus presenting a canoe appearance to an onlooker.

4 Fish Swimming

This is an under-water version of the canoe, but in this case the back should not be hollowed.

5 Propeller

Take up the horizontal floating position. Scull with the hands beyond the head so as to drive water away from it. The action must be confined to the rotation of the hands about the wrist, without bending the elbows. The body will travel feet first, and the direction can be controlled by sculling with one hand or the other.

6 Torpedo

Adopt the horizontal floating position again. Hollow the back and press the head backwards and at the same time commence sculling vigorously with the hands beyond the head. The body will then travel feet first, at an angle to the water surface. The head being pressed back and the back being hollowed, only the feet will appear above the surface. Point the toes so as to give the impression of the torpedo 'head' cutting through the water. For both the Torpedo and the Propeller, initial velocity can be obtained by floating on the back, sculling with the hands by the sides, and then throwing the arms over to the position above the head. This requires a good deal of practice, and it is better to delay this until the actual propulsion is achieved first from the normal horizontal floating position.

7 Pendulum Floating

Take up the horizontal floating position. Slowly bring the straight arms in line with the shoulders at right angles to the body and raise the head gently, so causing the feet to sink. As the feet pass the vertical, the arms are taken forward, followed by the head, so as to bring the face downward between the arms. The feet will then rise behind, thus bringing you to the *prone* floating position. Next, reverse the head and arm movements to swing the body back through the arc to the starting position. The body must be kept in as straight a line as possible throughout, without bending at the hips.

8 Oyster

Take up the horizontal floating position. Keep the arms straight and pressed against the head. Bend the body quickly at the hips, swinging the arms over—still pressed against the head—until the fingers touch the toes. The body will then spin forwards, with the back breaking the water surface, as in the Mushroom float, and the fingers and toes, still touching, will point directly downwards. Straighten the body out quickly to the prone floating position, and then roll over on to the back, which is the starting position again. The whole movement is then repeated several times.

9 Marching on the Surface

First of all, you should practise this movement with the hands sculling gently by the sides, in the back floating position. Propel the body, feet first, by alternate movements of the legs as in walking. Bend at the knee, so as to draw the lower leg and foot under the body vigorously, thus exerting a pressure between it and the body. Carry out the reverse movement of straightening the knee-joint in a gentle manner or else the effect of the initial movement will be cancelled out. Later, place the hands on the hips, or cross them over the chest. Keep the knees under the surface and do not splash in any way.

10 The Water Wheel

Lie on one side of the body, with the upper arm and hand resting on the hip and the under arm bent, with the hand against the ear. Use the legs to walk round in a circle on the surface.

11 The Corkscrew

Commencing on the bottom of the bath with the above-mentioned Water Wheel position and movement, the body will rise to the surface in a corkscrew or spiral movement. This is a very effective manoeuvre when it is carried out quickly.

12 Washing Tub

From the back sculling position, double up the body into a sitting position, with the knees turned outwards and in

F

line with the chin. Cross the legs and use the hands as for sculling, one pushing water away from the body and the other towards it. The body will then spin in whichever direction is chosen.

13 Spinning Top

Take up a vertical float position, with the arms folded. Push with one foot and pull with the other as quickly as possible. This action will cause the body to revolve on a vertical axis.

14 Backward Somersault

Take up the horizontal floating position and then draw up the legs to the body, with the knees against the chest. As the feet are lifted, drop the head backwards, and with the hands beside the body, push downwards with the palms towards the bottom of the bath. This will cause the feet to come out of the water and the body to turn over backwards.

15 Forward Somersaults

Tread water in the vertical position. Draw up the knees close to the chest and raise the arms sideways in line with the shoulders. Drop the head forwards and move the arms forwards, downwards, and upwards like a scoop, causing the body to rotate. Once started, the arm movements can be continued for successive somersaults.

16 Backward Full-Length Somersaults

Take up the horizontal floating position, with the arms extended beyond the head. Hollow the back and depress the head and arms below the surface. Cup the hands and make rapid pulling movements towards the surface. Continue this action until the starting position is attained again. Keep the eyes open so as to note direction and progress relative to the bottom of the bath and to the surface.

17 *Forward Full-Length Somersaults*

Take up the prone floating position, with the arms extended beyond the head. Bend the head forwards, and make a 'breast stroke' sweep with the arms, as for a surface dive. As the body reaches the vertical, the head bent forward will cause it to rotate, and the hands can hasten the movement with a further downward pressing action.

18 *Rotating and Revolving on the Surface*

For this skill, the hands and legs are not used in any way, but are kept extended; the legs are pressed together at the ankles and the thumbs are locked in the horizontal floating position. The movement is started by a tensing of muscles along the side of the body in the direction of the desired revolution. The body will then travel in a circle with the feet as centre, since the shoulders, being wider than the feet, will travel further for each rotation. About twenty complete revolutions of the body will be required to complete the full circle.

19 *Rolling Log*

The starting position for this is exactly the same as that for the previous movement, but the body should roll along a straight line. To achieve this, you should think of the action of a rolling log. Any tendency to turn to one side is counteracted by pushing back the shoulder on that side for each revolution. This again is an entirely muscular effort, starting all down one side of the body.

20 *Submarine*

Start by sculling in the supine position, raising one leg vertically to the body. If, however, this proves too difficult, bend the knee so as to bring it over the chest, with the lower leg and toes pointing straight into the air. Move along the surface feet first. Then, to dive, reverse the palms and scoop the water inwards towards the body and upwards towards the surface. To surface again, the palms are reversed, and quick sculling will bring the body up again. Breathing takes place while you are travelling along the surface.

21 Spiral Surface Dive

Perform a surface dive in the normal manner, and when the body is vertical, you can cause it to revolve by pressing the hands alternately from left to right or right to left. It is necessary to exert some downward pressure, as well as lateral, to slow down the body, so that a full spiral turn can be made before the feet disappear under the surface.

22 The Crab

Starting from the prone floating position, the body is caused to move sideways by pressing the hands alternately from left to right or right to left. The legs, sprawled apart like the arms, carry out a similar movement.

23 Plunging

This is no longer a competitive event for A.S.A. Championships, but it is a useful adjunct to a racing dive. The body takes up its starting position with the feet slightly apart on the bath side, toes gripping the edge. The body is then bent forward from the hips, with knees bent and arms stretched to a position which can vary from 45 degrees in front of and below the shoulders to a similar position behind the shoulders. The arms are swung forwards and upwards; the body rises on to the toes and is launched forward to enter the water shallowly to the surface, but not flat on the surface. A full inhalation is made as this is done, and the body travels along the surface, driven by the thrust obtained from the feet pushing off from the side. The body should not rotate in any way, and the face must be fully submerged. A time limit of 60 seconds was imposed when Plunging was a competition event. The head position controls the depth of the initial entry, and this should be a normal position between the arms as they are swung upwards. Once in the water, the back should be hollowed slightly, and the heels should just break the surface as the body drifts along in a completely relaxed condition.

Having acquired a fair degree of skill in the various swimming strokes, the pupil may now wish to test his prowess against that of his friends. With this desire to swim quickly comes the need for further study of how to win a swimming race. This involves a knowledge of at least two skills—how to start and how to turn at the end of the bath in the shortest possible time. Let us now consider these two skills separately.

C Racing Starts

The initial phase of all starts, with the exception of back crawl, is exactly the same. The differences between the various strokes occur after the swimmer has left his mark and is under the water. Bearing this in mind, we will first discuss the Initial Phase.

The Starter will indicate your position behind the starting line, and from that moment you are under his orders. He will then call 'Take Your Marks,' when you should take an easy step forward to assume the following position on the edge of the bath. Your feet should be hip-width apart, with the toes overlapping the edge of the bath to provide a good take-off and to prevent you from slipping. Ankles and knees should be slightly bent and your body leaning forward almost to the point of over-balancing. The head is relaxed, following the natural curves of the body. The arms may either hang down or be held back in rear of the thighs. When the starter is satisfied that all the competitors are quite still and ready, he will give the starting signal, and your object then is to get moving as quickly as possible.

Spring out as far as you can, throwing your arms forward and stretching your body, legs and feet to make them streamlined, so that you enter the water like a javelin. It may help you to develop the idea of this stream-lined entry if you lock your thumbs together the moment they enter the water.

One important point to remember is—do not try to 'breast' the surface of the water, but rather try to dive without a splash. At the moment of entry, the body should be rigid, and as straight as possible. This position must be held until such time as the tremendous drive obtained from the dive starts to slow down. This plan is normally known as 'the glide.' It is after the glide that the different techniques for each stroke are used; we will now deal with each of these in turn.

1 *Breast Stroke*

The fact that it is possible to swim breast stroke faster under water than on the surface suggests that we might take some advantage of this in the racing start. However, the Laws of the A.S.A., with which we must comply, say that not more than one arm stroke and one leg kick may be taken under water.

The depth of dive is usually about three feet. As momentum from the dive starts to slow down, take a wide sideways and downwards pull with the arms to bring the hands to the thighs. The arms then recover by keeping the hands as close to the body as possible and pushing them forward in front of the face to the glide position. As the hands pass the face going forward, one good leg kick is made. This will drive the body forward and upward to the surface. Care must be taken not to start a second stroke until the head has broken the surface.

2 *Butterfly*

The Laws state that 'the arms must recover over the

surface of the water,' but they do not restrict the number
of leg kicks which may be taken when under water. The
pattern of this start is the same as breast stroke until the
completion of the glide. As momentum is lost, keep the
arms stretched forward and start your leg action going,
in order to drive you forward and upward. As you
approach the surface, take a large sideways and downwards
pull with the arms; once the hands reach the thighs,
swing the arms forward *over* the water and start the full
stroke.

3 Front Crawl

The depth of this dive is usually about two feet, not quite
as deep as the breast or butterfly strokes. Once again the
body is kept streamlined until momentum starts to die.
The leg thrash is then started to bring the body to the
surface. In order to assist in the return to the surface, one
arm pull is taken after the leg thrash has started. This
should bring you to the surface so that the arm recovers
over the water and you can go straight into the full stroke.

4 Back Crawl

In the back crawl the start, of course, is in the water.
When the starter calls you to 'take your marks,' grasp the
rail with both hands, about shoulder-width apart. The
feet are brought up on to the wall, just under the surface
of the water, about hip-width apart. Some swimmers
prefer to have one foot higher than the other one, with the
toes of the lower foot level with the heel of the upper one.
Either of these foot-placing methods may be used.

The body is now in a tightly tucked position, with the
hips close to the heels and the buttocks above the surface
of the water. On the starting signal being given, throw
your arms over your head and push off as vigorously as
possible. This will throw your body out over the surface
of the water in a stretched position, with the body slightly

arched. As you enter the water, keep this arched position, so that you make a clean-cut entry. Keep the body stretched and straight, with the arms extended above the head, and glide under water. Once you start to lose the momentum gained from your push off the wall, start the flutter kick first and then follow on with the full arm stroke.

D Racing Turns

For distances over one length, the competitor who can turn about quickly after touching has a considerable advantage over his less able opponents. In consequence, a close study of the ways and means of effecting quick turns for the various racing strokes will well repay the would-be competitor.

(a) The Breast Stroke Turn

The approach should be made at full speed, and to comply with the rules, the touch on the bath side must be made with both hands simultaneously. Until the actual moment of touching, the body must be maintained in a level position, without being allowed to roll or twist.

As the hands touch, allow the elbows to bend so that the face comes close to the wall. Simultaneously with the touch, the body tucks up and the head is raised; this will cause the body to drop, seat first, under the water. Immediately the body swivels either to the left or to the right. In order to assist this swivel action, turn the head sharply and scull with the opposite hand. This will also assist in keeping your body close to the wall. Keeping the knees bent and apart, place them firmly on the wall. The arms then move forward and the head is lowered between them; as the head comes between your arms, immediately straighten your legs and drive the body forward under the water. Once again the body is stretched out and remains straight and still during the glide. As momentum starts to die, execute the one arm pull and leg kick as described in the 'Breast Stroke Start'.

Remember that to comply with the laws, the body must be on the breast when the push-off from the wall takes place, and the head must break the surface before the second arm pull takes place.

(b) The Front Crawl Throw-away Turn

The 'throw-away turn' is the simplest of the front crawl turns and is the one generally used in the middle distance races. As in all turns, the approach is made at speed, and the touch is made with one hand. As soon as you touch tuck the body up and turn on to the side of the touching hand. As you tuck up, lift the head and allow the feet to sink. The free hand performs a sculling action which assists in turning the body round and keeps it close to the wall. The touching hand is now taken off the wall and thrown overhead, to join the free hand which is now stretching forward. Keep your knees bent and place them firmly on the wall. Now lower your head between your arms and, by straightening the legs, drive the body out under the water. Again stretch out for the glide. The transition from the glide to the full stroke is the same as previously described in the 'Front Crawl Start'.

(c) The Half-turn Back Somersault Turn

Most of our fastest swimmers today when sprinting use a different turn from the 'swivel' called the 'sprint' or 'somersault' turn. As its name implies, this turn is an actual under-water somersault performed in the following manner. As the swimmer approaches—at full speed, of course—and when within a yard or two of the wall, he rolls over on to his back and hits the wall with one hand, fingers pointing downward. By using this hand and arm as a kind of lever, he throws his head backward and starts a backward somersault, tucking up the legs and knees to the chest. Continuing his turn until his feet come in contact with the wall of the bath, he then pushes off with a glide as in the swivel turn.

(d) The Back Crawl Turn

There are three different methods used for this turn. The easiest—and the one which is best learned first because it serves as a useful introduction to the other two—is the spin turn, with the head kept out of the water.

Method I

Spin Turn with Head out of Water—This turn in its main essentials is practically the same as the front crawl swivel turn, except that the body is the other way up. The touch is made with one hand, the knees are tucked up, and the body is swung round until the feet come to rest on the wall. From this position, the feet drive hard against the wall to propel the body into its under-water glide.

Method II

Spin Turn with Head under Water—The difference between this and the previous turn lies in the angle or direction of the turn which, instead of being more or less horizontal, becomes rather more vertical. In other words, it is more of a somersault than a horizontal twist, the head being taken much deeper in the water. This fact enables the legs to be lifted out of the water and consequently, because drag is lessened, adds greatly to the speed of the turn. As in the first method, the arms are used to control the turn, and at the time of the actual push-off, they should have taken up their position fully stretched behind the head in readiness for the back glide.

Method III

The Half-Somersault Turn—In order to comply with the rules governing back-stroke competitions, it is necessary that the body at no part of the turn shall be completely face-down in the water. Thus if one were to attempt a complete back somersault turn as described for the front crawl, disqualification would result. The expert competitor surmounts this problem, however, by making a *half* somersault, and when he is approximately upside down, that is, feet up and head down, he makes a sideways twist to bring himself into position for his push-off as in the two previously described methods. This turn is practically the same as the second method, except that the head is carried deeper in the water and the somersault part of the turn is a vertical rather than a horizontal spin.

(e) *The Butterfly Turn*
The approach, touch, turn and glide are the same as already described for the Breast Stroke Turn. However, to comply with the rules, the transition from glide to full stroke must conform to that previously described in 'The Butterfly Start.'

Summary
It is fully realised that the average reader of this book will not be able to perform the many water skills which have been described in this chapter. The object of inserting them all is merely to offer a number of suggestions as to how the reader can relieve the somewhat monotonous work and practice which is necessary if he is to become expert at the various swimming strokes which have already been described. Every one of these skills, however, will also develop confidence, and that—as has already been pointed out frequently in this book—is one of the major essentials in learning to swim.

So these water skills serve the double purpose of giving pleasure and fun on the one hand, and steadily increasing confidence on the other hand. You will probably find that a few of them come naturally to you, whereas others are difficult or even impossible. Do not worry about that, because it is better to be able to perform three or four of these water 'tricks' really well than it is to do most of them badly and untidily. So have a shot at them all, and then concentrate on the ones which seem easiest to you personally.

CHAPTER X

Water Polo

Let us now assume that you, the reader of this book, have taught yourself to swim with the help of the many suggestions in the foregoing chapters. There are at least two excellent ways in which you can utilise this ability; one is a game—water polo—and the other is a very practical form of service to the community—life-saving. This chapter is concerned with the recreational aspect, water polo, a grand game which develops determination, courage, skill and stamina. Yet it is only fair to admit at once that it is a 'tough' game when it is played seriously. While much fun can be had by a number of beginners playing 3- or 4-a-side in an ordinary pool with improvised goals and almost any kind of ball, the main object of this chapter is to explain the chief principles of water polo so as to give the reader a general but fairly comprehensive idea of what to expect when he watches or plays the real game.

The rules for water polo have been laid down by the Federation Internationale de Natation Amateur, and, subject to certain interpretations and rulings, these rules have been adopted by the Amateur Swimming Association. The game is played in a rectangular pool with seven players on each side and a minimum depth of one metre of water. The length of this rectangle may vary between 20 and 30 metres, while the width may be anything from 8 to 20 metres; these variations obviously allow for considerable differences in the sizes of pools. The field of play is crossed by seven imaginary lines, as shown in the following diagram:

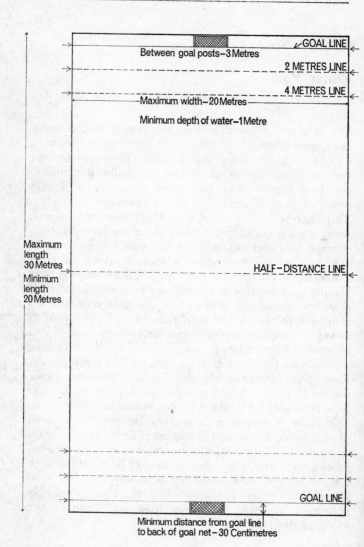

GOAL LINE

Between goal posts – 3 Metres

2 METRES LINE

4 METRES LINE

Maximum width – 20 Metres

Minimum depth of water – 1 Metre

Maximum length 30 Metres

Minimum length 20 Metres

HALF – DISTANCE LINE

GOAL LINE

Minimum distance from goal line to back of goal net – 30 Centimetres

The ends of the imaginary lines are shown by distinctive marks, which must be clearly visible throughout the game. The distance between the inner sides of the goal-posts is 3 metres, and the minimum distance from the goal line to the back of the net is 30 centimetres. The goal-posts and the crossbar must be made of wood or metal, with rectangular sections of 0·075 metres, square with the goal line and painted white; they must be in front of any obstruction. The underside of the crossbar must be 0·90 metres above water surface when the water is 1·50 metres metres or more in depth, and 2·40 metres from the bottom of the bath when the depth of the water is less than 1·50 metres.

The ball is the same size as an ordinary soccer ball, with a circumference of not less than 0·68 metres and not more than 0·71 metres. Its weight must be between 400 and 450 grammes, and it must be fitted with a self-closing valve. The referee, who must have ample room to move along the side of the bath, must be provided with a stick 70 cms. long, fitted with a white flag on one end and a blue one on the other, each flag to be 35 cms. by 25 cms. Similarly, each of the two goal judges must be provided with a red flag and a white one of the same size, but mounted on separate sticks 50 cms. long.

For the sake of clarity when they are in the water, one team must wear dark blue and the other team white caps; but as the goalkeepers have special functions and privileges, they must wear red caps. The caps are tied with tapes under the chin, and they are numbered as follows: Goalkeeper, No. 1; Left Back, No. 2; Right Back, No. 3; Half-Back, No. 4; Left Forward, No. 5; Centre Forward, No. 6; Right Forward, No. 7.

The officials normally consist of a referee, a timekeeper, a secretary, and two goal judges. It is necessary for the referee's whistle to be a shrill one, so that it can be heard by the players above the shouts of the spectators or when their heads are submerged while swimming. An 'advantage rule', similar to that in use in all other ball games like soccer, rugger and hockey, gives the referee authority not to sound his whistle for a foul if, in his opinion, such an action would be to the advantage of the offending team. The timekeeper must also have a shrill whistle, in addition to an accurate stop-watch; he whistles for half-time and full-time independently of the referee. The goal-judges take up their positions on the opposite side of the bath to the referee and directly level with the goal-line; their duties are to signal with a white flag for a goal-throw, with a red flag for a corner-throw, and with both flags for a goal.

The actual duration of a game of water polo is 20 minutes, in four periods of five minutes each. The teams change ends before commencing each new period, between which there is an interval of two minutes. The Secretary must be fully acquainted with the Rules of Water Polo, and his duties include the recording of penalty points awarded. He must be stationed near the timekeeper, and he must announce to the referee each third penalty point awarded against either team, because at that stage a Penalty Throw must be awarded to the opponents.

The timekeeper must stop his watch for all stoppages in the game, such as when the ball goes outside the field of play, or when there is an accident, or when the referee calls for the ball out of the water. Each of these stoppages may be only a few seconds' duration, but added up they may lengthen a game by several minutes. Before the start of a game, the two captains toss for choice of ends; the loser, incidentally, has the choice of caps. Each captain should see that his players are wearing no articles likely to cause injuries, and that their bodies have not been rubbed with oil or grease, because offending players are liable to be ordered out of the water and only re-admitted after inspection by the referee.

The game is started—and re-started—by the players taking up positions about one metre apart on their respective goal-lines; when the referee is satisfied that both teams are ready, he blows one sharp blast on his whistle and releases or throws the ball into the centre of the field of play. The game then goes on, like any game of soccer or hockey or basket-ball, with the players inter-passing and dribbling and shooting, until the ball goes out of play or until the referee's whistle sounds. If an attacking player sends the ball over his opponents' goal-line, the defending goal-keeper is awarded a 'goal-throw'; but if a defending player sends it over his own goal-line, he concedes a 'corner throw' to his opponents. When a corner throw is taken, no players except the defending goal-keeper are allowed inside the 2 metre area.

Water polo is a fast game played by 14 swimmers in a comparatively small area, and there is so much congestion at times that fouls are fairly frequent. Fouls are divided into two categories—'ordinary fouls' and 'major fouls'. The rules give a list of 17 ordinary fouls; common ones are: starting before the referee blows his whistle, holding on to the rails, pushing off from the sides, walking when play is in progress, splashing in the face of an opponent, touching the ball with both hands at the same time, and impeding an opponent who is not holding the ball. For all these and similar 'ordinary fouls,' the penalty is a free throw to the nearest opponent, to be taken where the foul occurred. The only exception to this is when the foul is committed within the two-metres area; the free throw must then be taken from the two-metres line opposite the point at which the foul occurred.

'Major Fouls' include such things as holding, sinking, or pulling back an opponent when not holding the ball. In addition to a free throw to the opposing side, a penalty point is awarded to the non-offending team. In very serious cases, the referee has power to order a player to retire for the whole game. The referee indicates a foul by blowing his whistle and exhibiting the flag corresponding in colour to the caps worn by the non-offending team.

In the case of certain fouls committed by the defenders inside their 4-metres line, the referee may award a 'penalty throw'. The player who has been fouled is then given the opportunity of a free shot at goal from any point on the 4-metres line, with only the defending goal-keeper to beat; all other players must leave the 4-metre area. The player scores direct from a penalty throw, but if the ball rebounds from the goal-posts or crossbar, it must not be played by him again until some other player has touched it.

From the foregoing account, the reader will probably have gained a fairly comprehensive idea of the objects of the game of water polo. Yet no written account can compensate for the real excitement which the game itself provides, and any reader who has reached the stage where he is seriously considering taking up water polo should seize the first opportunity of going to watch a game. If you can manage to go with a friend who is able to answer the many questions which will spring to your mind, so much the better; but once you have reached such a stage, you are really stepping out beyond the scope of this book, and it only remains for me to wish you good luck as you begin to apply the knowledge we hope you have gained from it.

CHAPTER XI

Life Saving

Every person who is able to swim reasonably well can—
and should—be capable of saving the life of someone in
danger of drowning. Yet there is a vast difference between
ordinary swimming and the modern specialised strokes
developed for life saving; and the keen swimmer, especially
one who has taught himself, will not be completely satisfied
until he has mastered these proper methods of rescue—
and after that, of resuscitation.

Artificial Respiration

Two hundred years ago, the method of inducing artificial
respiration was to insert the pipe of a pair of bellows into
one nostril and, after closing the other, to pump air into
the lungs and then expel it by pressing the chest. Later, a
method of 'rolling' the patient from side to face downwards
was introduced; then, for a longer period, the 'face downwards' position was generally accepted as the best. Let
us consider this question of artificial respiration before we
deal with the problems of actually rescuing a drowning
person from the water.

The Royal Life Saving Society, 14 Devonshire Street,
London W.1, publishes (for 4/6d, including postage) a
splendid little booklet of instruction which contains everything the would-be life saver ought to know and all
swimmers should possess a copy of it. It is essential to
realise that respiration, or the act of breathing, consists of
two distinct acts—inspiration and expiration. Inspiration,
or breathing in, is produced by muscular actions which

enlarge the thorax so that extra supplies of air are drawn in to the lungs through the windpipe. Expiration, or breathing out, is mainly produced by the resilience of the lungs, thorax, and abdomen, causing the pressure inside the lungs to rise and forcing out air through the nose and mouth. Even after a normal expiration, however, the lungs still retain a large amount of air. This can in part be expelled by pressure upon the thorax and abdomen; on relaxing such pressure, air again enters the chest.

It is on this fundamental feature that Sir Sharpey Schafer's method of artificial respiration, the Holger Nielsen method, and the more recent Silvester-Brosch method all rest. Whatever method is used, however, it is essential that artifical respiration should be given as quickly as possible.

The Expired Air Method of Artificial Respiration

The method may be carried out by any one of three techniques. These are (a) Mouth-to-Nose, (b) Mouth-to-Mouth, or (c) Mouth covering nose and mouth of the patient (for use with small children and babies).

The patient is placed on his back and his head tilted fully backwards by placing one hand under his neck and the other hand on top of his head. When maximum tilt has been achieved, the hand under the neck is moved to the patient's chin, the thumb between the lips and the chin, the index finger following the line of the jaw and the remaining fingers curled into the palm of the hand. Care must be taken not to press on the throat. Whilst carrying out this positioning, the operator must take deep breaths and also carry out a brief inspection of the mouth to ensure that there is no obvious blockage of the air passages. The operator then opens his mouth wide, makes an airtight seal over the nose of the patient and blows. The thumb of the hand holding the chin can be used to seal the lips. He turns his head, after blowing, to watch for chest movement and at the same time inhales deeply, ready for the next blow into the patient's nose. If the chest does not rise, he checks that the patient's mouth and throat are free of obstructions. If air enters the patient's stomach through blowing too vigorously, he presses the stomach gently with the patient's head turned to one side. This is less likely to occur when using the mouth-to-nose technique than with the mouth-to-mouth as the nose acts as a natural reduction valve. The mouth-to-mouth technique is used when the patient's nose is blocked but if used in preference to the mouth-to-nose when the nose is not blocked, the nostrils must be sealed with the operator's cheek or the hand moved from the top of the head and the fingers used to pinch the nostrils to prevent an escape of air through the nose. The wrist should be kept low down on the forehead to ensure that the full tilt of the patient's head is maintained.

Resuscitation is commenced with ten quick inflations to give rapid build-up of oxygen in the patient's blood and then continued at a rate of twelve to fifteen respirations per minute.

With small children and babies, the operator seals his mouth over the nose and mouth of the patient and inflates at a rate of twenty per minute using a series of puffs, each one ceasing as the chest STARTS to rise. UNDER NO CIRCUMSTANCES BLOW VIOLENTLY INTO A BABY'S LUNGS.

Although the method can be carried out following the description given above, it is strongly recommended that a proper course of instruction from the Royal Life Saving Society or one of the first-aid societies is undertaken.

Safety Precautions

On the simple principle that prevention is better than cure, it is worth while considering some of the common circumstances which lead to a risk of drowning, and which, if at all possible, should be avoided. One of the most dangerous is the use of rubber floats and air beds by children—or even by adults—in the open sea, without some method of control against wind or tidal action. The modern development of sailing as a pastime has brought in its wake the urgent necessity for all regulations to be scrupulously obeyed, especially as regards the wearing of buoyancy equipment. It must be strongly emphasised, too, that swimming alone is in itself a danger, especially where there may be hidden rocks or steeply shelving shores or banks. It is somewhat surprising that statistics show that drownings in rivers and streams are more numerous than those in the sea; this is probably due to the fact that more people are rescued from the sea, especially at holiday resorts which have special facilities to assist bathers.

In a list of safety instructions, the Royal Life Saving Society advises swimmers not to strike out too far at right-angles to the shore or bank, but to swim parallel to it, so that help will always be closer at hand. The old warning—'do not swim too soon after a meal'—is still applicable, while the ever-increasing use of modern underwater swimming apparatus requires special training, especially if a supervisor is not available. It is a mistake, also, to remain in the water too long, particularly in cold conditions.

The Actual Rescue

There is no need in a book of this kind to enumerate and describe the various methods of release and rescue which are recommended by the R.L.S.S., but a few general hints and suggestions may not be out of place. It is a moot point whether or not the rescuer should remove some of his clothing before he enters the water. If the drowning person is on the surface and close to the shore, the rescuer will probably be in the water for a very short time, and under such circumstances there would be no need to remove much clothing. All the same, it is advisable in a general sense to remove as much clothing as time will permit, especially heavy garments and boots.

Recovery from the Bottom

To recover a submerged body, it is necessary for the rescuer to dive from the surface of the water. Having reached a point immediately above the victim, the rescuer, swimming the breast stroke, takes a full breath as his legs make their sweep in the rear, and then depresses his head and shoots his hands together towards the bottom. He then uses his arms to make a vigorous breast stroke. This, combined with a movement of the hips which causes his legs to rise almost vertically out of the water, will drive him down to a considerable depth. He should keep his eyes open to assist his search.

A point to remember is that while in still water bubbles rise perpendicularly, they will rise obliquely in running water, so that the rescuer must search higher up stream for the actual body. Once the victim has been found, he should be seized by the head or under the armpits. The rescuer's left foot should then be placed on the ground and his right knee in the small of the drowning person's back. Then, with a vigorous push from the bottom, the rescuer will be able to reach the surface by using the back-stroke leg movement.

When the patient is conscious and breathing normally and his ability to swallow has been tested by a few drops of warm water, a little hot tea sweetened with plenty of sugar may be offered to him. He should then be laid on his side in a warm bed, raised at the foot so that the head is slightly lower than the body to send as much blood as possible in the direction of the brain. He should be encouraged to sleep, and must be carefully watched for several hours to see that breathing does not again fail.

Further details about life saving are beyond the scope

of this book. If the reader has become interested in the subject, he can always follow it up by taking one of the examinations of the R.L.S.S. and obtaining such awards as a Certificate, Bronze Medallion, Bronze Cross, or Award of Merit. If he does so, he will undoubtedly render a great service to the community and, perhaps, help to bring about a decrease in the number of lives lost every year by drowning. With what better thought could the writer bring a book such as this to a close?